Conversational Navajo Workbook

An Introductory Course for Non-Native Speakers

A topical approach to learning Navajo with simplified grammatical explanations.

Everyday conversational patterns for teachers, counselors, and health-care providers

Garth A. Wilson

Conversational Navajo Workbook

Garth Wilson

ISBN 0-938717-54-5

Garth Wilson
Pinon Ridge Rd. (7-11)
Blanding, UT 84511

INTRODUCTION

The goal of the Conversational Navajo Workbook is to introduce you to the basic structure of the Navajo language without a lot of linguistic jargon. This workbook is only the beginning to your study and mastery of the Navajo language. Patterns are introduced that present grammatical concepts in a topical format.

The Conversational Navajo Workbook is designed to be not only a course text, but also a self-study guide. Each lesson begins with a list of relevant vocabulary that will be used in everyday conversational patterns. Grammatical explanations have been kept to a minimum, presenting only concepts that facilitate your understanding and use of the language. Grammatical concepts are summarized in a box for easy reference. Following the patterns or grammatical concepts are practice exercises that allow you to develop your language skills. Practicing the questions both orally and in writing will help you build fluency and retain what you have learned.

There are two main sections in the Conversational Navajo Workbook. The first section is the Pronunciation Guide. This section is designed to help you in learning the phonology system of the Navajo alphabet. The Pronunciation Guide Audio Cassette will help you to accurately pronounce Navajo words.

In the second section are the twenty topical lessons that present new vocabulary and concepts. The Workbook Audio Cassette provides a pronunciation model for the vocabulary and practice questions.

The Conversational Navajo Workbook was designed to be used in conjunction with the Conversational Navajo Dictionary, a pocket-sized, quick reference guide that includes a topical appendix for teachers, counselors, and health-care providers. The dictionary is simply organized to assist both the beginning and advanced speaker of Navajo.

CONTENTS

PRONUNCIATION GUIDE

Yá'át'ééh! Welcome to the Conversational Navajo Pronunciation Guide. The exercises in this section are specially designed to help you build accurate pronunciation, reading, writing, listening, and comprehension skills in the Navajo language. You probably have heard that Navajo is a very difficult, almost impossible, language to pronounce. Let me put your mind at ease! Yes, it is different in some ways than English. However, as you will find, there are more similarities in the sounds, or what are called phonemes, between English and Navajo than there are differences. A real practical help to you in learning Navajo is that Navajo, unlike English, is written phonetically.

Let me introduce you to the organization of the pronunciation guide. Each new pronunciation skill will begin with an explanation, followed by several examples. The skill will be summarized in easy-to-remember terms and found in the rectangular box.

Following the explanation, you may find two types of practice exercises. In the first exercise, you will find nonsense syllables that exclusively concentrate on the pronunciation skill being learned. It is suggested that you listen to these syllables, then say them *outloud*. When you feel confident in pronouncing these syllables, move on to the next exercise.

The next exercise will be a list of carefully selected words that practice the skill being learned. Again, listen to the word and then pronounce it *outloud* enough times that you can approximate the pronunciation fairly closely. Brief definitions are provided for your information only.

Finally, each pronunciation skill will have a mastery check to help you know how you are doing. To do this, first pronounce the word *outloud*, then listen to the tape to check your pronunciation. Review as needed. Your goal should be to fluently (smoothly and naturally, not hurried) approximate the correct pronunciation as closely as possible.

1

When a person learns English as a second language, he has the difficult problem of coordinating spelling and pronunciation. For example, **gh** is "silent" in words like throu**gh**, ni**gh**t, and thou**gh**t. But it is "f" in words like lau**gh**, tou**gh**, and rou**gh**. Another example is **a**. Notice the different sounds **a** has as you pronounce f**a**t, f**a**te, f**a**ther, and **a**bout.

In learning Navajo you are more fortunate. The words are pronounced exactly as they are written. **S** is always pronounced "s"; **b** is always "b", and so on. Until the early 1900's there was no written language; when linguists wrote down the language, they used letters and symbols that correspond exactly to the Navajo sound system.

NAVAJO-ENGLISH SOUND EQUIVALENTS

Navajo	English	Navajo	English
b	**b**oy	ts	ha**ts**
d	**d**oor	m	**m**ad
t	**t**ime	n	**n**ot
k	**k**ite	l	**l**ike
kw	**qu**ick	w	**w**ood
g	**g**o	y	**y**es
ch	**ch**air	a	f**a**ther
j	**j**oy	e	l**e**t
h	**h**ave	i	b**i**t
s	**s**o	o	g**o**
z	**z**oo	ee	**the**y
sh	**sh**e	ii	**see**
zh	plea**s**ure		

Some Navajo sounds, however, have no English equivalent: *tł, t', ts', k', ch'*.

Practice
1. *Study the Navajo-English equivalents by pronouncing outloud the Navajo letter and the corresponding English sound equivalent.*

Mastery Check
Mastery is achieved when you can accurately pronounce he Navajo sound while covering up the English column.

VOWELS - A, E, I, O

Navajo	English
a	father
e	let
i	bit
o	go

Examples: shash (bear)   sin (song)
              tsé (rock)   sho (frost)

Practice

1.   Pronounce the following nonsense syllables outloud.

a. chi	b. sha	c. cha	d. she	e. che
ja	se	zi	ji	ye
le	wa	lo	ya	li
mi	yo	so	ne	zo
no	za	ma	we	wo

f. sho	g. cho	h. shi
si	ze	yi
na	ni	me
je	jo	wi
mo	la	se

2.   Pronounce the following words outloud.

a. abid (stomach)   f. gah (rabbit)
b. sis (belt)   g. gad (juniper)
c. awos (shoulder)   h. sodizin (prayer)
d. shash (bear)   i. dikos (cough)
e. sin (song)   j. nahalin (it resembles)

3

LONG VOWELS - AA, EE, II, OO

Navajo	English
aa	ja**w**
ee	th**ey**
ii	s**ee**
oo	s**o** (like *o* but held out longer)

Examples: s**aa**d (word; language) s**ii**l (steam)

bee (by means of him) d**oo**da (no)

Practice

1. *Pronounce the following nonsense syllables outloud.*

a.	choo	b.	shaa	c.	chee	d.	chii
	saa		wee		yii		moo
	yee		zoo		laa		yaa
	nii		jii		woo		zee
	loo		maa		see		lii

e.	shee	f.	shaa	g.	shoo	h.	shii
	waa		naa		yoo		noo
	joo		soo		zaa		mee
	sii		wii		mii		jaa
	nee		jee		lee		zii

2. *Pronounce the following words outloud.*

baa (about it) naadiin (twenty)

biih (into it) nee (concerning you)

4

dooda (no)	Hoozdoh (Phoenix, Az.)
saad (word)	bizaad (their language)
bee (concerning it)	doo (it will be)
yiikah (go forward)	atiin (road)
biniinaa (because)	hastiin (man)

Mastery Check

Pronounce the preceding list of words outloud, then check your pronunciation by listening to the tape.

VOWEL TONE - HIGH (´) VS. LOW

Navajo vowels (and the consonant "n") can take on either of two tones --high or low. The high tone is indicated by a "high mark" (´) over the letter.

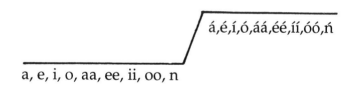

á,é,í,ó,áá,éé,íí,óó,ń

a, e, i, o, aa, ee, ii, oo, n

Examples: dibé (sheep)   ádin (it is absent; nothing)

tseebíí (eight)   hóla (I don't know)

Practice

1. *Pronounce the following nonsense syllables outloud.*

a. siiló	b. lééwo	c. zéná	d. jeeno	e. siisíí
nóóno	yozáá	naanii	zoolá	yeelá
leelé	zíílo	zólí	niiwíí	wóno
mámii	moonéé	yoojí	láájo	jójo
jajá	sééwa	wíloo	málii	maasi
yéloo	wooyé	nowéé	móóyaa	jíjee

5

2. *Pronounce the following words outloud.*

a. dibé (sheep)
b. chidí (car)
c. bééhózin (it is known)
d. ákondi (however)
e. abíní (morning)
f. diné (people)

g. wolyé (it is named)
h. naniné (you are playing)
i. hóla (I don't know)
j. shijáád (my leg)
k. ádin (it is absent)
l. golchóón (quilt)

Mastery Check

Pronounce the preceding list of words outloud. Then listen to the tape to check your pronunciation.

VOWELS - ORAL VS. NASALIZED (˛)

Vowels can be either oral or nasalized. **Oral vowels** are made by letting the air pass through the mouth (oral cavity.) **Nasalized vowels** are made by letting the air pass through the nose (nasal cavity) as well as the mouth.

Below are pairs of English words. One word of each pair contains an oral vowel while the other contains a nasalized vowel (the nasalized vowels in English come before a nasal consonant--"m," "n," or "ng"). Say each pair aloud and listen carefully to the difference between the two vowels.

Oral	Nasalized	Oral	Nasalized
bob	bǫmb	hit	hįnt
call	cạlm	did	dįm
debt	dęnt	fold	phǫne
head	hęm	hope	hǫme
ick	įnk	bake	bạnk
seed	sęem	bog	bǫng

6

Nasalized vowels in Navajo are indicated by the nasal mark ( )
underneath the vowel. When a vowel precedes a nasal consonant ("m"
or "n"), it is automatically nasalized, so the nasal mark is not written.
For example, in the word *adláanii*, the **áa** is nasalized, but the nasal
mark isn't written. Except for this case, a vowel with no mark under it
is oral.

*Whether a vowel is oral or nasalized can make a difference in the
meaning of the word.*

Examples: biih - into it   shí - I
              bįįh - deer   shį́ - summer

A nasal mark (ˌ) under a vowel indicates that
it is nazalized. A vowel with no nasal mark is
oral.

Examples: bąą (because of it) dį́į́' (four)
              sęęs (wart)   yishchǫǫh (I am
                                              ruining it)

Practice

1. *Pronounce the following nonsense syllables outloud.*

a. mą	b. jo	c. mǫǫ	d. nįį	e. mįį
shą	lį	jąą	zii	zęę
la	wǫ	wąą	lęę	wee
ję	cho	sǫ	yęę	yąą
nę	sį	loo	wįį	jęę

f. sąą	g. ji	h. jǫǫ
nǫ	chį	jį
chaa	shǫǫ	nąą
lą	zįį	męę
jįį	wę	ze

2. *Pronounce the following words outloud.*

a. bįįh (deer)

b. bąą (because)

c. bizęęs (his wart)

d. yishchǫǫh (I'm ruining it)

e. sizį́ (she is standing)

f. jį́ (day)

g. shį́ (summer)

h. shį́į́ (probably)

i. hólǫ́ (it exists)

j. halą́ (confusion)

k. ílį́ (valuable)

l. nahalǫǫ (it resembles it)

Mastery Check

Pronounce the above list of words, then check your pronunciation by listening to the tape.

CONSONANTS - Ł, TŁ

ł	Place your tongue in a position as if to make an "l" sound. Then blow out.
*tł	A "t" released into an "l" as in telegraphy, telepathy

*These two letters together present *one sound*. Whenever you see them together, don't think of individual letters--think of the sound they represent.

Examples: łeh (usually)   ditłéé' (it is wet)

nohłį́ (you are)   tłah (ointment)

Practice

1. *Pronounce the following nonsense syllables outloud.*

a. ał	b. áł	c. aał	d. ááł	e. ąął
oł	ół	ooł	óół	ǫǫł
ił	íł	iił	ííł	įįł
eł	éł	eeł	ééł	ééł

2. *Pronounce the following nonsense syllables outloud.*

a. ło	b. łoo	c. bił	d. woł
sho	łii	bish	wosh
la	shii	neeł	jash
łe	łi	neesh	jał

3. *Pronounce the following nonsense syllables outloud.*

a. tłi	b. tłee	c. gla	d. tłaa
tła	glii	tła	tło
gla	tłii	glee	tłoo
tłe	tło	tłee	tła

4. *Pronounce the following words outloud.*

a. tłah (ointment)
b. bił (with it)
c. łeh (usually)
d. ditłéé' (it is wet)
e. łid (smoke)
f. łóód (a sore)
g. niiltłah (it stopped)
h. dideeshtłił (I will light it)
i. nihił (with us)
j. nishłį (I am)
k. didíłtłił (you will light it)
l. shił (with me)

Mastery Check

Pronounce the preceding list of words outloud Then check your pronunciation by listening to the tape.

9

GLOTTAL STOP (')

Say aah. . .

Compare the air coming out from your lungs to water coming through a hose. If you could squeeze the hose at any point, the water would stop. The same thing is true of the air coming from your lungs through your mouth.

If you stop the air with your lips you produce the sound of a "p" or a "b". If you stop it with the tip of your tongue it would be a "t" or a "d". With the back of your tongue it would be a "k" or a "g" (as in "gun").

There is one more place (believe it or not) farther back to stop the air--the glottis. The stopping of air with the glottis is called a *glottal stop*. The glottal stop is used as any other consonant in Navajo and is represented by the symbol (').

' Sound made by stopping the air with the glottis as in "oh'oh," "butler" (bu'ler), or "hu', two, three four!"

Examples: shizhé'é (my father)   ła' (one, some)
            e'e'aah (west)   łóó' (fish)

Practice

1.   *Pronounce the following nonsense syllables outloud.*

a. ła'	b. zhe'e	c. zo'	d. łoo'
ne'	łá'ąą	be'	na'
ti'	íʼíí	yee'	łe'e
wa'	le'e	shaa'	ki'i
sho'	o'o	chii'	jo'

10

e. a'aa	f. she'e	g. woo'	h. ła'
ge'	ba'a	e'aa	te'
nii'	lo'oo	ii'ą	choo
so'	łi'i	ą́ą́'ą́	wi'á
ni'	he'e	o'óón	na'

2. *Pronounce the following words outloud.*

a. na' (here)	e. e'e'aah (west)	i. dine'é (people)
b. ge' (be quiet)	f. ha'a'aah (east)	j. éé' (clothes)
c. łóó' (fish)	g. lą́'ąą (fine)	k. bitoo' (stew)
d. łį́į' (horse)	h. i'íí'ą́ (evening)	l. ba'aan (in addition)

Mastery Check

Pronounce the above list of words out loud. Then check your pronunciation by listening to the tape.

GLOTTALIZED CONSONANTS - T', K', CH', TS', TŁ'

Navajo has a set of consonants, called *glottalized consonants,* which are closely related to other consonants.

Look at the relation between the two sets below.

t	k	ch	ts	tł
t'	k'	ch'	ts'	tł'

Since you already know how to say *t, k, ch, ts,* and *tł,* you can almost pronounce the glottalized series. All that remains to be added is the glottalization.

To produce the glottalized consonants, **follow explicitly** these instructions.

---

1. Hold your breath (i. e., stop the air with your glottis)

2. Still holding your breath, say *t* repeatedly, but do not release the air from your glottis. It is crucial that you hold your breath as you produce the *t*.

3. Release your breath before you pass out.

4. Repeat the steps above with *k, ch, ts,* and *tł.*

Note: Remember that the combinations of the letters *t', k', h', ts',* and *tł'* represent one sound. Whenever you see them together, don't think of the individual letters, but of the sound they represent.

Examples: t'áá (just)   ch'iyáán (food)
           tsits'aa' (box)   át'é (it is)
           ts'ídá (very, really) k'ad (now)
           bik'eh (according to him) tł'óół (rope)
           nantł'ah (it is difficult) ch'ah (hat)

Practice
1. *Pronounce the following nonsense syllables outloud.*

a. t'o	d. k'e	g. ch'o	j. ts'o	m. tł'o
b. t'a	e. k'a	h. ch'i	k. ts'a	n. tł'i
c. t'i	f. k'i	i. ch'e	l. ts'e	o. tł'a

2. *Pronounce the following nonsense syllables outloud.*

a. tin	d. kad	i. chin	n. tsin	s. tłah
b. t'aa	e. k'in	j. chał	o. tsi	t. tł'i
c. t'eeł	f. ko	k. ch'ii	p. ts'iid	u. tłoh
d. toh	g. k'e	l. ch'ǫ	q. tsah	v. tł'e
e. tal	h. ke	m. chee	r. ts'e	w. tłooł

3. *Pronounce the following words outloud.*

a. ch'ał (frog)
b. t'óó (just)
c. k'aa' (arrow)
d. át'é (it is)
e. ch'ah (hat)
f. k'ad (now)
g. t'áá'aaníí (truly)
h. ch'iyáán (food)
i. ts'aa' (basket)
j. ts'ídá (really)
k. ts'in (bone)
l. bik'i (on it)
m. ak'áán (flour)
n. nantł'ah (it is difficult)
o. atł'aa' (rump)
p. bik'eh (according to it)
q. t'áá (just)
r. ch'osh (bug)
s. tł'óół (rope)
t. ts'ah (sage)
u. nishtł'ah (left-handed)
v. bits'iiní (she is skinny)
w. ch'ééh (in vain)
x. hwiit'į́ (we've seen it)
y. atł'ó (she is weaving)

Mastery Check

Pronounce the above list of words outloud. Then check your pronunciation by listening to the tape.

DIPHTHONGS

Two or more different vowels sometimes combine to form one sound, called a *diphthong*. Examples in English are "b**oa**," tr**ia**l," and "**oi**l."

> For example: a + o = ao (as in **ou**ch)
> ah-oh

Navajo	English
ai	Haw*ai*i
a o	T*ao* s
ei	n*ei*ghbor
oi	che*wy*

Practice

1. *Pronounce the following nonsense syllables outloud.*

a. bai	c. nai	e. sei	g. dai
dao	jei	toi	tłei
dai	lao	tłoi	sao
chao	woi	tsei	tai
łai	mei	shoi	tsoi

b. ch'ei	d. k'ai	f. shei	h. łei
nao	t'ei	ch'ao	tł'ei
ts'oi	doi	ts'ai	ch'oi
mai	choi	t'oi	ts'ao

2. *Pronounce the following words outloud.*

   a. deesdoi (it is hot)
   b. hait'áo (how)
   c. beeldléí (blanket)
   d. éí (that)
   e. haigo (winter)
   f. t'óó'ahayóí (many)
   g. choiniil'į́ (we use it)
   h. séí (sand)
   i. daolyé (they are called)
   j. ádaohłééh (you make it)
   k. háísh (who)
   l. át'áo (being)

Mastery Check

Pronounce the above list of words outloud. Then check your pronunciation by listening to the tape.

14

G, H, K, T

The pronunciation of the consonants *g, h, k,* and *t* depends upon the vowel that follows them. Before *e* and *i*, certain of these consonants are followed by a *y* sound.

For example: ké is pronounced kyé
                 tį' is pronounced tyį
                 nihí is pronounced nihyí

Before *o* certain of these consonants are followed by a w sound.

For example: tó is pronounced twó
                 hóla is pronounced hwóla
                 kodi is pronounced kwodi

The following chart shows which vowels and consonants the *y* or *w* sound occurs with. A dash means that no change occurs.

	VOWELS			
	a	e	i	o
g	-	y	-	w
h	-	y	y	w
k	-	y	-	w
t	-	y	y	w

*Following *g, h,* and *k,* the *w* sound is rather slight.

Practice

1. *Pronounce the following nonsense syllables outloud.*

a. ge	b. ki	c. to	d. ge	e. hi
he	gi	ho	gi	he
ke	hi	ko	go	ho
te	ti	go	gi	he
he	hi	to	ge	hi

f. ti	g. go	h. he	i. gi	j. ge
to	hi	ki	ki	go
te	ko	to	gi	he
ti	te	go	ki	hi
te	gi	ke	gi	ho

k. ko	l. ke
ke	ko
ki	te
ko	ti
ke	to

2. *Pronounce the following words outloud.*

    a. ké (shoes)

    b. tį' (let's go)

    c. nihí (us)

    d. tó (water)

    e. gohwééh (coffee)

    f. hooghan (home)

    g. damóogo (on Sunday)

    h. góó (to)

    i. bikéyah (their land)

    v. nahałtin (it is raining)

    w. béégashii (cows)

    x. agaan (arm)

    y. doodago (or)

    z. atoo' (stew)

    aa. tódiłhił (whiskey)

    bb. yéigo (diligently)

    cc. mandagíiya (butter)

    dd. kin (building)

j. łikan (it is sweet)

k. hóla (I don't know)

l. ahééh (gratitude)

m. t'áá'áko (o.k.)

n. hóló̜ (it exists)

o. ashiiké (boys)

p. kodi (here)

q. yá'áhoot'ééh (nice area)

r. bikee' (his shoes)

s. ákondi (however)

t. tin (ice)

u. ahéhee' (thank you)

ee. go (suffix as)

ff. hózhó̜ (happiness)

gg. at'ééké (girls)

hh. hóyéé' (dangerous)

ii. dahiistł'ó̜ (rug or loom)

jj. gi (suffix at)

kk. hágo (come here)

ll. łigai (it is white)

mm. télii (donkey)

nn. bééhózin (it is known)

oo. kóne'é (in here)

Mastery Check

Pronounce the above list of words outloud. Then check your pronunciation by listening to the tape.

GLIDING VOWEL SOUNDS

When two vowels of differing tone are together a *gliding tone* is produced.

Examples:

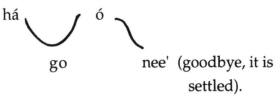

há ⌣ go   ó ⌇ nee' (goodbye, it is settled).

The *o*'s have a rising tone.

só
bi ⌒ odi (pig)

The *o*'s have a falling tone.

17

> A gliding tone (rising or falling) is produced when two vowels of differing tones are together.

Practice

1. *Pronounce the following words outloud.*

   a. áadi (there)
   b. naat'áanii (leader)
   c. łitsoósh (yellow?)
   d. bisóodi (pig)
   e. hágoónee' (good bye)
   f. ákoósh (so?)
   g. bilagáana (Anglo)
   h. yiską́ągoósh (tomorrow?)

   i. t'áadoo (don't)
   j. béeso (money)
   k. yéigo (diligently)
   l. niísh (you?)
   m. háadi (where?)
   n. díidí (this one)
   o. naakiísh (two?)
   p. ńléidí (that one)

Mastery Check

Pronounce the preceding list of words outloud. Then check your pronunciation by listening to the tape.

GH

The pronunciation of the consonant "gh" depends on the vowel that follows it. First we will learn how to pronounce "gh" when it is followed by "a." Place your tongue in position to produce a "g" sound in English. Then drop your tongue slowly and let the air force through the passage in the back of your mouth.

Below are some words containing the sound:

hooghan - hogan, home   aghaa' - wool

Before the vowels "e" or "i," "gh" is *most* like a "y" sound in English. In most modern literature (including this book), when "gh" is followed by "e" or "i," the word is spelled with "y."

Examples: aghe' = aye'   - son
                  naalghéhé = naalyéhé   - merchandise
                  Dighin = Diyin   - God; it is holy

Before the vowel *o,* "gh" is *most* like a "w" sound in English. In recent books, when "gh" is followed by "o," the word is spelled with "w."

Examples: ghohcha = wohcha   - you (2) cry
                  gholghé = wolyé   - he is called it

In *gha, gh* is produced by pushing air through a passage between the tongue and the far back of the roof of the mouth.

In *ghe, gh* sounds like *y.*

In *ghi, gh* sounds like *y.*

In *gho, gh* sounds like *w.*

Practice

1.   *Write the modern spelling of the following words in the blanks provided.*

     a. ghołbéézh _____   f. bighi'   _____

     b. aghaa'   _____   g. hooghan _____

     c. ghóshdę́ę́' _____   h. gholghé _____

     d. yinishghé _____   i. adiilghoł _____

     e. ghołchǫǫh _____   j. ghohcha _____

2. *Pronounce the following words outloud.*

   a. hooghan (home)
   b. baghan (his home)
   c. dah diníilghaazh (fry bread)
   d. bá hooghan (house for it)
   e. naaghá (he is walking)
   f. Tségháhoodzání (Window Rock)

   g. bighá (through it)
   h. Dziłghá'í (Apache)
   i. bighaa' (its wool)
   j. Ghąąji' (October)
   k. aghaa' (wool)
   ·l. nilghaał (he is chewing it)

Mastery Check

Pronounce the above list of words outloud. Then check your pronunciation by listening to the tape.

DL, DZ, TS and ZH

The Navajo symbols represent the corresponding sounds in English. Each symbol, although it is a combination of two letters, represents *one sound*. Whenever you see the symbol, don't think of the individual letters it contains, but of the sound it represents.

Navajo	English Equivalent
dl	Delilah, deliver
	a**d** lib (a-**dl**ib)
dz	ai**ds**, loa**ds**, a**dz**e
ts	bi**ts**, lo**ts**, ha**ts**
zh	a**z**ure, lei**s**ure,
	plea**s**ure

Practice

1. *Pronounce the following nonsense syllables outloud.*

a. dla	b. dzá	c. tsin	d. zhą
dlo	dzee	tsal	zhi'
dlił	dzi	tse	zhee
dlee	dzoł	tso	zhon
dla	dzaan	tsił	zhel

2. *Pronounce the following words outloud.*

a. łizhin (black)	m. azhé'é (father)
b. łitso (yellow)	n. iidlą́ (we two are drinking)
c. adláanii (a drunk)	o. bideezhí (younger sister)
d. adziilii (power)	p. bidziil (he is strong)
e. asdzáán (woman)	q. Na'nízhoozhí (Gallup)
f. ashdla' (five)	r. t'áá'ałtso (all of them)
g. atsį' (meat)	s. nizhóní (it is pretty)
h. ashą́ (I am eating)	t. t'áá'áníidla (both of us)
i. bi'niidlí (he is cold)	u. tsin (stick)
j. atsilí (younger brother)	v. Tódínéeshzhee' (Kayenta)
k. bidziil (he is strong)	w. dlǫ́ǫ́ (prairie dog)
l. Tségháhoodzání (Window Rock)	x. atsii' (hair)

Mastery Check

Pronounce the above list of words outloud. Then check your pronunciation by listening to the tape.

GLOTTAL STOPS BEFORE INITIAL VOWELS

A vowel at the beginning of a word is called an *initial vowel* (e.g., **á**din, **a**díílwoł). When an initial vowel follows the final vowel of another word, a sound change occurs. Try to discover this sound change by looking at the examples below:

shíká + adíílwoł	shíká'adíílwoł (you help me)
nihee + ádin	nihee'ádin (we don't have any)
shi + éé'	shi'éé' (my clothes)
dóó + ałníí'	dóó'ałníí' (and half)

As you can see, when an initial vowel follows a final vowel, a glottal stop is spoken (but not written) between the two. In many other books, the glottal stop is written before every initial vowel (e.g., 'ádin, 'adíílwoł).

> **When an initial vowel follows the final vowel of another word, a glottal stop is inserted between the two vowels.**

Practice

1. *Write each of the following pairs of words together, putting in the glottal stop where it is spoken.*

Example:	yah iit'aash	yahiit'aash
	baa áhwiilyá	baa'áhwiilyá

a. t'áá áko	_____	e. yaa áhalyá	_____
b. shee ádin	_____	f. t'áá íídą́ą́'	_____
c. bee adziilii	_____	g. dah asdáhí	_____
d. yah ooh'aash	_____	h. bíká adíílwoł	_____

2. *Pronounce the following phrases outloud inserting the glottal stop(s) where needed.*
   a. dibé nihee ádin (we don't have sheep)
   b. áłchíní baa áhashyá (I am taking care of children)
   c. nihíká adíílwoł (you will help us)
   d. shíká anilyeed (you help me)
   e. t'áá aaníí (truly)

f. bee óhólnííhii (authority)

g. doo ąą át'ée da (it is not open)

h. díí éiyá (this)

i. nihinaaltsoos ąą ádaohłééh (open your books)

j. nihilį́į́' baa ádahołyą́ (take care of your animals)

k. shíká adíílwoł (you will help me)

l. baa ahééh daniidzin (we are thankful)

Mastery Check

Pronounce the above list of phrases outloud. Check your pronunciation by listening to the tape.

VOICED VS. VOICELESS CONSONANTS

There is a distinction between certain consonants in Navajo that will help us to understand a particular sound change that occurs with them. Try to discover this distinction by feeling your vocal chords as they say the following pairs of sounds out loud.

zh - sh

z - s

Notice that your vocal chords vibrate when you say "zh" or "z" but they don't vibrate when you say "sh" or "s." Consonants like "zh" and "z" are called *voiced consonants*; consonants like "sh" and "s" are called *voiceless   consonants*. Voiced and voiceless consonants occur in pairs, such as "zh - sh" and "z -s." Now try to determine which consonant is voiced and which is voiceless in the pairs below, again by saying them out loud and feeling your vocal chords.

Voiced - Voiceless	Voiced - Voiceless
z - s	gh - h
zh - sh	l - ł
d - t	g - k

23

```
┌─────────────────────────────────────────────────────────┐
│                                                           │
│   VOICED                                                  │
│   CONSONANT:        Consonant produced                    │
│                     *with* the vocal chords               │
│                     vibrating.                            │
│                                                           │
│                                                           │
│   VOICELESS                                               │
│   CONSONANT:        Consonant produced                    │
│                     *without* the vocal chords            │
│                     vibrating.                            │
│                                                           │
└─────────────────────────────────────────────────────────┘
```

X

When the *h* sound follows *s*, it is written x to avoid confusion
with the symbol *sh*.

Examples: **yiyiis-hį** (he killed him) is written **yiyiisxį**

ni'diis-hį (you were killed) is written **ni'diisxį**

nás-héés (I am turning it around) is written **násxéés**

Note: the slight "y" sound found after h (see page 14) applies to the X.

Practice

1. *Pronounce the following words outloud.*

    a. shi'diisxį (it is killing me)

    b. sisxé (I am killing it)

    c. yiyiisxį (he killed him)

    d. nídeesxis (I will turn it around)

    e. néísxiz (he turned it around)

    f. ni'diisxį (it is killing you)

    g. shiisxį (it killed me)

    h. łitsxo (it is orange)

Mastery Check

Pronounce the above list of words outloud. Then check your pronunciation by listening to the tape.

FINAL H

Often the sound *h* occurs at the end of a syllable or word, following a vowel. In this position, it is like the sound you make when you blow into your cupped hands to keep them warm on a cold day. Listen to words containing a final *h* compared to words without this sound.

naah'aash
- You (2) are walking around.

naa'ash
- They (2) are walking around.

dooh'ash
- You (2) will go.

doo'ash
- They (2) will go.

n'dínóohtįįł
- You (2) will teach.

n'dínóotįįł
- They (2) will teach.

adoohdlíįł
- You (2) will drink.

adoodlíįł
- He will drink.

Notice that the final *h* often makes a difference in meaning between two words. Many beginners when learning Navajo frequently leave out this sound. The following practice exercises will help to develop the final *h* sound so you will be better understood and sound more like a native speaker.

Practice

1. *Pronounce the following sets of words outloud.*

    a. adootł'óół
        adoohtł'óół

    b. didooniił
        didoohniił

    c. doo'ash
        dooh'ash

    d. naa'aash
        naah'aash

    e. adoodis
        adoohdis

    f. naané
        naahné

    g. yidoodląął
        yidoohdląął

    h. naakai
        naahkai

25

2. *Pronounce the following words outloud.*

a. ła'ts'áadah (eleven)
b. łahda (sometimes)
c. áłah aleeh (meeting)
d. áshįįh łikan (sugar)
e. nantł'ah (it is difficult)
f. ahééh (gratitude)
g. dah sidá (it is sitting)
h. bik'eh (according to it)
i. bitah (among them)
j. dloh nízin (he feels like laughing)

k. áchį́įh (nose)
l. binahjį' (through it)
m. dééh (tea)
n. łeh (usually)
o. ch'ééh (in vain)
p. bilah (his friend)
q. e'e'aahgo (west)
r. aláahdi (greatest)
s. ch'ah (hat)
t. bááh (bread)

3. *Pronounce the following words outloud.*

a. dooh'ash
b. ńdaahkah
c. t'ahdii
d. didoohniił
e. wódahgo
f. naahné
g. ha'a'aahdę́ę́
h. yá'át'ééhgo
i. adoohdis
j. doohchah

k. bik'eh dohdleeh
l. k'ehjí
m. naahkai
n. naah'aash
o. adoohtł'óół
p. łahda
q. adoohdis
r. yidoohdlą́ą́ł
s. adoohdlį́į́ł
t. wóyahdi

Mastery Check

Pronounce the above list of words outloud. Then check your pronunciation by listening to the tape.

26

LESSSON 1 GRAMMAR PREVIEW

VOCABULARY

yá'át'ééh	- hello; it is good
hágoónee'	- goodbye; it is settled
haash	- what?; it what way?
yinishyé	- I am called it
yinílyé	- you are called it
wolyé	- he is called it

■ PATTERNS

The above vocabulary words can be used in simple greetings and farewells. Look at the pattern demonstrated below:

Question:	<u>Haash</u> yinílyé?	-What are you called? (What is your name?)
Answer:	<u>John</u> yinishyé.	- I am called John. (My name is John)

Notice that the interrogative *haash* in the question is replaced by the answer *John* in the reply. Unlike English that often changes word order in asking and answering a question, Navajo maintains the same word order or what is known as syntax. Note also that the verb to be called changes for the subject to preserve Subject-Verb agreement. Here are a few other examples of how this may be used in conversation:

Question:	Haash wolyé?	-What is she called?
Answer:	Jane wolyé.	-She is called Jane.
Question:	Haash wolyé?	-What is he called?
Answer:	Bill wolyé.	-He is called Bill.

The above verb, NAMED, TO BE, is found on page 89 in your Conversational Navajo Dictionary. There you will find a more complete conjugation of the verb with another example sentence.

■ PRACTICE

Answer the following questions.

1.   Haash yinílyé?   _____

2.   Haash wolyé?   _____

3.   Ask and respond orally to the above questions at least five times.

■   ACTION SENTENCES - SUBJECTS, VERBS, AND OBJECTS

Now that we've learned a basic pattern, let's look at examples of action sentences and the individual parts that make them up. First examine the simple sentence below:

Jane	ate.
SUBJECT	VERB

The two parts in this sentence are the <u>subject</u> "Jane" and the <u>verb</u> "ate". Notice that the subject is the person or thing in the sentence that is *doing* the action. In the corresponding Navajo sentence, the subject and verb are arranged in the same order:

Jane	ííyą́ą́'.
SUBJECT	VERB

Now look at a slightly more complex sentence.

Jane	ate	an apple.
SUBJECT	VERB	OBJECT

As you can see, this sentence contains one more part, the <u>object</u> "an apple". The object is what is *acted upon*, or the thing or person receiving the action of the verb. The corresponding Navajo sentence has the same three parts (subject, verb, and object), but in a **different order**.

Jane	bilasáanaa	yiyííyą́ą́'.
SUBJECT	OBJECT	VERB

Notice that in going from English to Navajo, the verb and object switch positions. Look at another example of this switch in word order.

Fred	bought	the pig.
SUBJECT	VERB	OBJECT

Fred	bisóodi	nayiisnii'.
SUBJECT	OBJECT	VERB

Word order in action sentences:	
<u>English</u>	<u>Navajo</u>
subject-verb	subject-verb
subject-verb-object	subject-object-verb

STATE-OF-BEING SENTENCES - SUBJECTS, VERBS, AND PREDICATE NOMINATIVES

Now that we've examined the major parts of an action sentences, let's look at a state-of -being sentence.

Joe Begay	is	a cowboy
SUBJECT	VERB	PREDICATE NOMINATIVE

Notice that the relationship between the parts of a state-of-being sentence is different than the relationship between the parts of an action sentence. In an action sentence, the subject *acts upon* the object. For example, in the action sentence, "Joe Begay hit a cowboy", Joe Begay acted upon a cowboy. In the state-of-being sentence above, however, the relationship between Joe Begay and the cowboy is one of equivalence (Joe Begay = cowboy). In this sentence, "a cowboy" is the predicate nominative. Look at the corresponding Navajo sentence.

Joe Begay	akałii	nilį́
SUBJECT	PREDICATE NOMINATIVE	VERB

Notice that it contains the same three parts as the English sentence, but the parts occur in a different order. In going from English to Navajo, the verb and the predicate nominative switch positions in the sentence. Here is another example of the sentence order.

This	is	a horse
SUBJECT	VERB	PREDICATE NOMINATIVE

Díí	łį́į'	át'é
SUBJECT	PREDICATE NOMINATIVE	VERB

> Word order in state-of-being sentences:
> | English | Navajo |
> |---------|--------|
> | subject-verb-predicate nominative | subject-predicate nominative-verb |

PARTS OF SPEECH - PREPOSITIONS AND POSTPOSITIONS

Next we will review another part of speech, the preposition and its accompanying phrase, the prepositional phrase. Look at the following examples:

We are learning <u>about</u> <u>Navajo grammar.</u>
preposition + object of the preposition = prepositional phrase

Harold works <u>for</u> <u>Mr. Johnson.</u>
preposition + object of the preposition = prepositional phrase

A prepositional phrase is a group of words like "about Navajo," "with me," or "under the table." As you can see, a prepositional phrase is composed of two parts--a preposition followed by an object of the preposition. Notice that both nouns and pronouns may functions as the object of a proposition. Look at the prepositional phrase below, paying special attention to the position of the preposition in relation to the object.

to	us
PREPOSITION	OBJECT

Notice that the preposition (pre-position) comes before the its object. The reason that ithis part of speech is called a "preposition" is because it is an a position preceding the object. Now look at how the phrase in expressed in Navajo. Again, pay special attention to the position of the the elements.

nihi-	ch'į'
(us)	(to)
OBJECT	POSTPOSITION

As you can see, there are no prepositions or prepositional phrases in Navajo. Taking their place are postpostions and postpositional phrases. In a postpostional phrase, such as the one above, the postposition (post-position) comes after its object. Here are a few more examples:

behind	the car
PREPOSITION	OBJECT

chidí	bine'
OBJECT	POSTPOSITION

beyond	it
PREPOSITION	OBJECT

bi-	lááh
OBJECT	POSTPOSITION

English	Navajo
Prepositional Phrase	Postpositional Phrase
Preposition-Object	Object-Postposition

■ PRACTICE

Rewrite the following prepositional phrases as a Navajo postpositional phrase.

1. Under the car _____

2. About the story _____

3. Toward me _____

4. With the teacher _____

5. Concerning her _____

◼ MORPHEMES

A morpheme is the smallest unit of meaning in a word. They are the building blocks with which words are formed. Look at the following English words divided into their morphemes:

> cats = cat + s (plural marker)
> teacher = teach + er (the one that does)
> players = play + er (the one that does) + s (plural marker)
> unclear = un (not) + clear

Some words contain only one morpheme.

Examples: elephant, people, sing, eleven, book, a, Utah

The words above cannot be broken down into smaller units of meaning. For example, if elephant were divided into el/e/phant, the three parts would have no meaning. El/e/and phant are syllables, or units of pronunciation.

By knowing morphemes and how they fit together, we can build words into new meanings. Look at the many different words that can be built with the small group of morphemes below.

<u>MORPHEMES</u>	<u>WORDS</u>
write	rewrite, writer, writing, writes, unwriteable, written

Navajo words, like English words, are composed of morphemes. In this workbook, we will study a number of mophemes that make up verbs, postpositions, and other parts of speech, as well as the rules on how they combine to form words.

> MORPHEME: basic unit of meaning.

◼ MORPHEME POSITION

Morphemes must always be put in the correct order when forming a word or else the word will not make sense. Examples: pre-school vs. school-pre, talk-ing vs. ing-talk, and un-clear vs. clear-un. Note that certain morphemes always occur at the end of a word. The position in which morpheme occurs is its morpheme position. Often we refer to morphemes by their position by calling them prefixes, suffixes, or infixes.

In Navajo, morphemes play an important part in building verbs and nouns. The following chart gives examples of how the Navajo verb is constructed using a series of morphemes. <u>Don't worry about memorizing each morpheme now</u>; it is not necessary to know all the parts of the verb to begin learning and speaking Navajo.

Position 10 - STEM
Position 9 - CLASSIFIER
Position 8 - SUBJECT MARKER
Position 7 - MODE AND ASPECT MARKER
Position 6 - ADVERBIAL MORPHEMES
Position 5 - DEITIC PRONOUNS (FOURTH PERSON IMPERSONAL)
Position 4 - DIRECT OBJECT
Position 3 - PLURAL MARKER
Position 2 - REPETITIVE MARKER
Position 1 - ADVERBIAL MORPHEMES (INDIRECT PRONOUN, REFLEXIVE,
               REVERSIONARY, SEMELITERATIVE)

Navajo verbs will usually use no more than seven of the above morphemes in building the meaning of the word; many will use only three or four morphemes. The stem in position 10 carries the meaning of the verb; the other morphemes indicates the who, how, and when of the verb. Note that the Navajo verb can convey a complete sentence, including the subject, object, indirect object, person of the subject, number of people involved, when, how, and meaning, and much more. Observe in the Navajo verbs below how it takes a whole sentence to express the same meaning in English.

MORPHEME POSITIONS

1	2	3	4	5	6	7	8	9	10
							ni	ł	béézh - You are boiling it.
na			nihi		ni		sh		tin - I am teaching you(pl)
á	ná	da		ji				d	dlįįh - They plural drink repetitively

Again, you should realize that it is <u>not</u> necessary to memorize all of the morphemes in the verb in order to begin learning and speaking Navajo. At first , your learning will primarily be memorization of verbs and nouns; later you will begin to incorporate phrases into your vocabulary. Then as you become able to communicate more freely, you will find that using and recognizing morphemes in your verbs happens rather intuitively.

■ CONJUGATING VERBS

Conjugating a verb means changing it to show who the subject of the verb is. In English, the subject is usually shown by pronouns <u>outside</u> the verb.

Example:
        I am playing, you are playing, he/she is playing, we are playing, they are playing.

In Navajo, however, the subject is usually shown by morphemes <u>inside</u> the verb. Therefore, when the subject of the verb changes, the internal form of the verb also changes. Notice the changes in the Navajo verb - PLAYING.

TO PLAY (see page 97 in Conversational Navajo Dictionary)

naashné I am playing	neii'né We (2) are playing	ndeii'né We (3 or more) are playing
naniné You (1) are playing	naahné You(2) are playing	ndaahné You(3 or more) are playing
naané He/She/They(2) are playing		ndaané They(3 or more)are playing

As you can see, Navajo verbs change internally more than English verbs do. Consequently, learning to conjugate verbs in Navajo is more important and complex than in English.

> Navajo verbs are conjugated (changed) to show who the subject of
> the verb is. The subject is indicated by morphemes within the verb.

■ PERSON

As you remember from the previous section, verbs in Navajo are conjugated to change who the subject of the verb is. To help us discuss the different forms of the verb that result from conjugation, we classify the forms according to person and number.

Example: TO BE, ROLE (see page 41 Conversational Navajo Dictionary)

PERSON

	SINGULAR	DUAL	PLURAL
1st PERSON	nishłį́ I am	niidlį́ **We** (2) are	daniidlį́ **We** (3 or more) are
2nd PERSON	nílį́ **You** (1) are	nohłį́ **You** (2) are	danohłį́ **You** (3 or more) are
3rd PERSON	nilį́ **He/She/They** (2) are		danilį́ **They** (3 or more) are

Person tells us whether the speaker is talking about self (I, We) in 1st PERSON, the person spoken to (You) in 2nd PERSON , or someone else (He/She/They) in 3rd PERSON. Nouns such as sheep, Robert, and Gallup are in the 3rd PERSON. Fortunately, there is no subjective or objective case such as I/Me, or We/Us, or She/Her, or He/Him in Navajo.

■ NUMBER

In relation to the subject of the verb, another way of classifying verb forms is according to NUMBER.   In English, verbs are either singular or plural.

Examples: SINGULAR   PLURAL

    I am   We are
    He runs   They run
    She studies   They study
    It goes   They go

There are several important differences between number in English and Navajo verbs. Try to discover the system of number in Navajo verbs by looking at the chart below, paying particular attention to information in the parentheses.

NUMBER

	SINGULAR	DUAL	PLURAL
1st PERSON	íínishta' I (1) am studying	ííníilta' We (2) are studying	da'ííníilta' We (3 or more) are studying
2nd PERSON	íínílta' You (1) are studying	íínólta' You (2) are studying	da'íínólta' You (3 or more) are studying
3rd PERSON	ólta' He/She/They (2) are studying		da'ólta' They (3 or more) are studying

Notice that in 1st person, Navajo verbs have a <u>singular</u> form (I - one), a <u>dual</u> form (we - two), and a <u>plural</u> form (we - three or more), depending on whether one, two, or three or more are participating in the verb as the subject. Similarly, in second person, there is a <u>singular</u> form (you - one), a <u>dual</u> form (you - two), and a <u>plural</u> (you - three or more). In third person, however, the situation is different. There is a <u>singular/dual</u> form (he/she - one, or they - two), and a <u>plural</u> form (they - three or more). With a few exceptions to this pattern, most Navajo verbs have a singular, dual, and plural forms in first and second persons, and singular/dual and plural forms in third person.

NUMBER IN NAVAJO VERBS			
	SINGULAR	DUAL	PLURAL
1st PERSON	1	2	3 or more
2ndPERSON	1	2	3 or more
3rd PERSON	1 or 2		3 or more

Note: In relation to the previous brief introduction to PERSON in verb conjugations, it should be noted that there are other forms of third person in which verbs can be conjugated. These verb conjugations are in the impersonal form and refer to "one or someone" without specifying who it may be. They are used in narrative, such as story telling, or in admonishment such as "one should not play with fire." Verbs in these third person impersonal forms are conjugated by using various morphemes in position 5.

■   ASPECT AND MODE

The Navajo language verb system uses two different ways of expressing meaning in the verb, namely, MODE and ASPECT. They are used to convey specific information about the action or event expressed in the verb. MODE differentiates the manner in which an action or event takes place. There are seven different modes in which a verb may be expressed. First is Imperfective, which expresses an incomplete action or event; second is Perfective, which expresses a completed action or event. Third is Progressive, which expresses an action or event that is on-going. Fourth is Usitative, which expresses an action or event that occurs regularly or customarily. Fifth is Iterative, which expresses an action or event that occurs repeatedly. Sixth is Optative, which expresses a desire or potential for an action or event to occur. And seventh, Future, which expresses actions or events or actions in the future.

ASPECT is somewhat different than MODE. ASPECT refers to the kind of action expressed. There are eight different ASPECTS in which a verb may be conjugated. First is Momentaneous, which expresses an action or event that takes place at a particular time. Second is Semelfactive, which expresses an action or event that only occurs once. Third is Punctual, which refers to the beginning of an action or event. Fourth is Repetitive, which expresses actions or events done is a series. Fifth is Continuative, which expresses actions or events that are continuing over a period of time. Sixth is Distributive/Diversative, which distributes the expresses action or event over a number of objects or events. Seventh is Reversative, which indicates an action or event that is reversed or turned around. And eighth is Conatative, which expresses the idea that the subject of the verb is attempting to perform the action or event of the verb.

Thoroughly confused? Rightly so. The Aspect, Mode, and Tense systems of any language are the most difficult to understand. Even linguists often leave these systems until last in studying a new language because it takes such a thorough understanding of the whole language in order to comprehend them. Do you understand the Aspect, Mode, and Tense systems in English? If you're an English teacher you might, otherwise you probably haven't even given it a thought. The systems briefly discussed above are included to introduce you to the complexity of the Navajo verb system. However, it is not necessary, or even expected, for you to memorize the various Modes and Aspects, let alone the numerous verbs that are conjugated within them.

In this workbook and in the Conversational Navajo Dictionary, you will be introduced to a number of commonly used verbs. Most of them will be conjugated in the Imperfective Mode. This mode is perhaps the easiest to learn initally, and has the broadest range of usefulness. For example in English: "I am writing a letter" is in the Imperfective Mode. You can put the word "writing" in the past tense by saying, "Yesterday I was writing a letter." That is not the same as saying "Yesterday I wrote a letter", but it conveys a similar meaning. Also, you could say, "Tomorrow I will be writing a letter". Again, that does not mean the same as, "Tomorrow I will write a letter", but when learning a new language, this type of circumlocution is a start.

As you become more fluent in conversation, you will find the need to more accurately express what you intend to mean. At that time you can begin to learn other Modes or Aspects such as Perfective, Future, or Repetitive. Being familiar with a broad range of verbs in the Imperfective Mode will enable you to easily learn other conjugations of the same verb.

■ CREATING YOUR OWN LEARNING SYSTEM

If you have a photographic memory, you may skip this section. For the rest of us, memorization is a process that allows us to recall information when the need arises. There are few things more discouraging and frustrating than to try and say something you've spent time learning and not being able to recall it. It is very possible for a non-native speaker of Navajo to become fluent in Navajo in many situations. Here are a few suggestions that many language students have used to avoid the short term memory trap.

1. Commit to learn something new every day.

2. Learn information by topics in a communicative situation. Picture situations where you want to communicate in Navajo. What do you want to say? What nouns and verbs would be helpful?

3. Write the verb conjugation and relevant nouns on a 3X5 card. Write a sample sentence or two that utilize these verbs and nouns in a pattern. Number the card in a sequence.

4. Practice outloud using the verb, nouns, and patterns over the next three days. Find opportunities to use it as much as possible. By the end of the three days you should know it very well.

5. Review the card a week later. Then review your cards monthly.

Let's say that today is the 93rd day you have been using your review system. Here are the seven cards you would be reviewing today:

Today's card - #93
Yesterday's card - #92
Two day's ago card - #91
Last week's card - #86
Last month's card - #63
Two month's ago card - #33
Three month's ago card - #3

Tomorrow you would be learning #94, so put #91 back in the file. Replace #86 with #87, #63 with #64, #33 with #34, and #3 with #4. Using this system will enable you to review everything at least once a month. More importantly, when you want to say something, you will be able to speak fluently without having to hesitate while trying to recall "that word".

LESSON 2 PRONOUNS AND STATE-OF-BEING VERBS

VOCABULARY

shí	- I, me	háí (sh, shą')	- who?
ni	- you (singular)	bá'ólta'í	- teacher
bí	- he/him, she/her, they, them, it	naat'áanii	- leader
nihí	- us, we	ayóó	- very
nihí	- you (plural)	íiyisíí	- really
bi'niidlí	- he is cold	t'áá íiyisíí	- really!
bi'ádíláah	- he is full of mischief		
biyooch'ííd	- she is lying		
bíhólnííh	- he is in charge		
bidziil	- she is strong		
bits'iiní	- he is skinny		
bijéékał	- she is deaf		

GRAMMAR

■ INDEPENDENT PERSONAL PRONOUNS

Look at the way independent personal pronouns are used in the sentences below.

<u>I</u> am learning Navajo.
<u>You</u> went home.
<u>She</u> washes her hair.
My mother gave <u>me</u> a present.
John talked to <u>them</u>.

Independent personal pronouns, as you can see, are pronouns (words that take the place of nouns) that refer to persons and occur by themselves. Below are the Navajo independent personal pronouns:

	SINGULAR	DUAL	PLURAL
FIRST PERSON	shí	nihí	*danihí
SECOND PERSON	ni	nihí	*danihí
THIRD PERSON	bí		*dabí

*Not frequently used.

37

These pronouns aften change when they become part of a verb or are attached to other words such as nouns or pronouns. For example: nihinaat'áanii - our leader (bí becomes low-toned)

Look at the sentences below to see one way independent personal pronouns are used:

Ni, haash yinílyé?   -You, what's your name?
Shí, Garth Wilson yinishyé.   -Me, my name is Garth Wilson.

Bí, haash wolyé?   -Her, what is her name?
Bí, Angie wolyé.   -Her, her name is Angie.

Notice that these pronouns are often used for emphasis -- they draw attention to the person.

■   PRACTICE

Fill the chart with the appropriate independent personal pronouns.

	SINGULAR	DUAL	PLURAL
FIRST PERSON			
SECOND PERSON			
THIRD PERSON			

■   STATE-OF-BEING VERBS

One small group of verbs are conjugated by changing the attached pronoun. These verbs, herein referred to as State-of-Being verbs, are also referred to as Passive verbs and Neuter verbs in other references. We will learn a number of these because they are easy to learn and will help us review the pronouns.

Observe how the following State-of-Being verbs are conjugated:

	SINGULAR	DUAL	PLURAL
1st PERSON	shidziil-I am strong	nihidziil-we are strong	danihidziil-we are strong
2nd PERSON	nidziil-you are strong	nihidziil-you are strong	danihidziil-you are strong
3rd PERSON	bidziil-he/she is strong		dabidziil-they are strong

Notice that the shi-, ni-, bi-, nihi-, danihi-, and dabi- are used to conjugate the verb -dziil are just like the independent personal pronouns except that they are <u>low-toned.</u>

Here are a few more State-of-Being verbs that conjugate in the same way:

bi'niidlí   - He is cold.
bi'ádílááh   - He is full of mischief
biyooch'ííd   - She is lying
bijéékał   - He is deaf
bits'iiní   - She is skinny
*bíhólnííh   - He is in charge

*Note: this pronoun is high-toned and often pronounced bóhólnííh. Not all plural forms are formed by simply adding "da" as a prefix.

◼ PRACTICE

A. Practice conjugating the State-of-Being verbs above until you can recite them from memory.

B. Translate the following sentences:

1. I am cold. _____

2. We (2) are lying. _____

3. She is strong. _____

4. Henry is in charge. _____

5. You (1) are full of mischief. _____

6. The leader is in charge. _____

7. You (2) are deaf. _____

8. Mary is skinny. _____

9. I am deaf. _ _____

10. They (3+) are strong. _____

11. We (2) are cold. _____

12. You (1) are lying. _____

13. Mike is full of mischief. _____

14. I am skinny. _____

◼ INTENSIFIERS

In the sentences below, look at the underlined words:
He really lies.
We are very cold.
I am extremely strong.
She is really in charge.

Words like "really", "very", and "extremely" are adverbs called intensifiers. The following are a few Navajo intensifiers:

ayóó   -very
íiyisíí   -really
t'áá íiyisíí -really!

Look at their position in the sentences below:

Ayóó nihidziil.   - We are very strong.
John íiyisíí bits'iiní   - John is really skinny.
Helen t'áá íiyisíí bóhólnííh   - Helen is really in charge.

Notice that intensifiers precede the verb in Navajo.

> Intensifiers are adverbs that precede the verb.

PRACTICE

Translate the following sentences:
1. Tanya is very cold. _____
2. John is really deaf. _____
3. The leader very lies. _____
4. The teacher is very skinny. _____
5. I am really deaf! _____
6. James is very strong. _____
7. The leader is really in charge. _____
8. Mark is very full of mischief. _____

INTERROGATIVES

An INTERROGATIVE is a word that asks a question. In English words such as who, where, what , and when are interrogatives. Look at how the interrogative hái (sh, shą') is used in the sentences below.

Háí ayóó bidziil?   Who is very strong?
John ayóó bidziil.   John is very strong.

Háísh biyooch'ííd?   Who is lying?
Shí, shiyooch'ííd.   Me, I am lying.

Háíshą' bi'niidlí?   Who is cold?
Nihí, nihi'niidlí.   Us, we are cold.

Because the subject of the verb is unknown, the interrogative *hái* replaces it to find out who the subject is. The reply (noun or personal pronoun) in turn replaces *hái*, just as the reply replaces *who* in English. Notice that *hái* is in third person, which requires the verb to be in third person.

> Háí (sh, *shą') is used like "who?" in English

*NOTE: the *sha'* enclitic (suffix) implies a slightly different meaning and therefore may be used in somewhat different situations. *Háísha'* implies the additional meaning of "which one of you out of a group". An example in English would be: A teacher asking the class, "Who wrote the dirty word on the chalkboard?" In combination with other interrogatives, the *sha'* may also imply a meaning of "what about - ".

■ PRACTICE

Ask and respond to the following questions both orally and in writing. In your answer, vary the response to reflect 1st person, 2nd person, and 3rd person. If an intensifier is used in the question, use it in the response.

Sample Question and Answer:
0. Háísh biyooch'ííd?   Shí, shiyooch'ííd OR
                        Ni, niyooch'ííd OR
                        Harry biyooch'ííd

1. Háí bidziil?_____

2. Háísh bits'iiní?_____

3. Háísha' bidziil? _____

4. Háí biyooch'ííd?_____

5. Háísh bóhólnííh?_____

6. Háísha' bi'niidlí? _____

7. Háí bijéékał?_____

8. Háísh bi'ádíláah?_____

9. Háísha' ayóó bidziil?_____

10. Háí íiyisíí bits'iiní?_____

11. Háísh t'áá íiyisíí biyooch'ííd?_____

12. Háísha' ayóó bijéékał?_____

13. Háí íiyisíí bóhólnííh?_____

14. Háísh t'áá íiyisíí bi'niidlí?_____

15. Háísha' ayóó bijéékał?_____

16. Háísh íiyisíí bi'ádíláah?_____

LESSON 3 YES-NO QUESTIONS

VOCABULARY

---

dooda	- no
ndaga'	- no
aoo'	- yes
dikos	- cough, cold
dichin	- hunger
dibáá'	- thirst
dikos bidoolna'	- he has a cough
dichin bi'niiłhį	- he is dying of hunger
dichin bi'niighą́ą́'	- they are dying of hunger
dibáá' bi'niiłhį	- she is dying of thirst
dibáá' bi'niighą́ą́'	- they are dying of thirst
at'ééd	- girl
ashkii	- boy
hastiin	- man
asdzáán	- woman
t'áá aaníí	- truly
dóó	- and

■ PRACTICE

1. Practice the vocabulary words and conjugating the State-of-Being verbs above until you can recite them from memory.

GRAMMAR

■ QUESTION MARKER - ísh

Compare the sentences below.

1.	Tarzan bidziil.	-Tarzan is strong.
2.	Tarzanísh bidziil?	-Is Tarzan strong?
1.	Ni'niidlí.	-You are cold.
2.	Ni'niidlíísh	-Are you cold?
1.	Ni.	-You.
2.	Niísh?	-You?

Notice that *-ísh/sh* is a question marker that is attached to the end of a word. If the word ends with a consonant (like Tarzan), -ísh is added. If it ends in a vowel (like ni'diiłá), that final vowel is lengthened and the *-sh* is added.

Different languages use various means of indicating that a question is being asked. In English we raise the tone of voice on the word(s) we intend to be the point of question. Often we also change the word order in a question. In Navajo, not only is the tone raised, but also utilizes an actual enclitic (suffix) - the high-toned *ísh/sh*. Korean and Japanese use a similar method of using a high-toned suffix.

The question markers *-ísh/sh* form questions that must be answered with a "yes" or "no". Below are words that can be used in a reply.

Aoo'	- yes
Ndaga'	- no
Dooda	- no

> *-ísh/sh* is a question marker that is attached to the end of a word. If it ends in a consonant, *ísh* is added; if it ends in a vowel, that vowel is lengthened and the *-sh* is added.

■ PRACTICE

Make each of the following statements into a question by adding the *-ísh* or the *-sh* as appropriate.

1. bi'niidlí _____

2. bi'ádílááh _____

3. biyooch'ííd_____

4. bijéékał _____

5. bits'iiní _____

6. bóhólníih_____

7. dikos bidoolna' _____

8. dichin bi'niiłhį _____

9. dichin bi'niighą́ą́' _____

10. dibáá' bi'niiłhį _____

11. dibáá' bi'niighą́ą́' _____

12. nidziil _____

43

NEGATING SENTENCES

To negate a sentence in English, we add "not" to it. For example:

I am skinny.   I am <u>not</u> skinny.

Look at how sentences are negated in Navajo.

1. Shiyooch'ííd.   - I am lying
   <u>Doo</u> shiyooch'ííd <u>da</u>.   - I am <u>not</u> lying.

2. Naat'áanii bi'ádííláah.   -The leader is full of mischief.
   Naat'áanii <u>doo</u> bi'ádííláah <u>da</u>. -The leader is <u>not</u> full of mischief.

3. Ashkii ayóó bidziil.   -The boy is very strong.
   Ashkii <u>doo</u> ayóó bidziil <u>da</u>. -The boy is <u>not</u> very strong.

Remember that *dooda* is one way of saying "no" in Navajo. To negate a sentence, split up dooda into *doo* and *da*; place *doo* before the phrase or word to be negated, and place *da* after it. If there is an intensifier in the sentence, the doo usually precedes it (as in example #3 above). Now look at negated verbs that end with a high toned vowel.

Doo shi'niidlíí da.   -I am not cold.

Notice that the vowel is lengthened and the second vowel is low. This is to enable the high toned vowel to round down to the low toned "*da*."

> To negate a sentence, place *doo* before the verb (and intensifier if present) and *da* after it. If the verb ends with a high toned vowel, the vowel is lengthened and the second vowel is low toned.

PRACTICE

Place *doo* before the following verbs and *da* following it, lengthening the final vowel where present.

1. _____bi'niidlí _____   6. _____t'áá íiyisíí bits'iiní _____

2. _____bidziil _____   7. _____bóhólnííh _____

3. _____ayóó bi'ádííláah _____   8. _____dikos bidoolna' _____

4. _____íiyisíí biyooch'ííd_____ 9. _____dichin bi'niiłhí _____

5. _____ayóó bijéékał _____   10. _____dichin bi'niigháá' _____

PATTERNS

Now that we have learned how to negate a sentence, it is time to put this concept into a pattern using questions and answers. In Lesson 2 the interrogative *háísh* (who) was introduced. This interrogative posed an open ended question. The *ísh/sh* question marker poses a question that must be answered with a yes or no, followed by an explanation.

Here are a few examples using vocabulary introduced in this lesson:

Question:	Hastiin dikos bidoolna'ásh?	- Does the man have a cough?
Positive Answer:	Aoo', hastiin dikos bidoolna'.	- Yes, the man has a cough.
Negative Answer:	Ndaga', hastiin doo dikos bidoolna' da.	- No, the man doesn't have a cough.
Question:	Asdzáánísh dichin bi'niiłhį́?	- Is the woman dying of hunger?
Positive Answer:	Aoo', asdzáán dichin bi'niiłhį́.	- Yes, the woman is dying hunger.
Negative Answer:	Ndaga', asdzáán doo dichin bi'niiłhį́į da.	- No, the woman is not dying of hunger.

As demonstrated in the examples above, first you answer the question with a yes or no, then go on to explain the answer.

PRACTICE

Translate the following questions, then answer them in both the positive and negative.

1. Is the boy very full of mischief?

Question: _____

Positive answer: _____

Negative answer: _____

2. Is the woman really deaf?

Question: _____

Positive answer: _____

Negative answer: _____

3. Does the girl have a cough?

Question: _____

Positive answer: _____

Negative answer: _____

4. Is the man dying of thirst?

Question: _____

Positive answer: _____

Negative answer: _____

45

5. Are the boy and girl dying of hunger?

Question: _____

Positive answer: _____

Negative answer: _____

6. Does the woman have a cough?

Question: _____

Positive answer: _____

Negative answer: _____

7. Are the man and the woman dying of thirst?

Question: _____

Positive answer: _____

Negative answer: _____

8. Who does not have a cough? (this is a review question asked in the negative.)

Question: _____

Answer:_____

9. Who is not really deaf?

Question: _____

Answer:_____

10. Who is not lying?

Question: _____

Answer:_____

11. Who is not very strong?

Question: _____

Answer:_____

12. Are you really dying of hunger?

Question: _____

Positive answer: _____

Negative answer: _____

13. Is the leader really in charge?

Question: _____

Positive answer: _____

Negative answer: _____

LESSON 4 GOING TO AND BEING FROM

VOCABULARY

-góó	- to
-déé'	- from
háágóó	- where to?
háádéé'	- where from?
ha'át'íí (sh, shą')	- what?
tsxį́į́łgo	- hurry!
áłtsé	- wait
tį'	- let's go
k'ad	- now
ch'ééh	- in vain
ólta'	- school, class
da'adání	- cafeteria
bá hooghan	- house for it
béeso bá hooghan	- bank (house for money)
da'iigis bá hooghan	- laundromat (house for washing)
naalyéhé bá hooghan	- trading post, general merchandise store
sodizin bá hooghan	- church (house of prayer)
naaltsoos bá hooghan	- bookstore

■ PRACTICE

Practice the vocabulary words outloud until you can recite them from memory.

■ PATTERN - TO BE GOING

The following verb TO BE GOING can be used to express going to a place. It is found on page 69 in the Conversational Navajo Dictionary.

	SINGULAR	DUAL	PLURAL
1ST PERSON	déyá	deet'áázh	deekai
2ND PERSON	díníyá	dishoo'áázh	disoohkai
3RD PERSON	deeyá	deezh'áázh	deeskai

Note: Unlike most verbs, GO VERBS are conjugated in both the 3rd person singular and dual forms.

47

Notice in the example patterns that the interrogative is replaced with the answer. Also note the **subject-verb agreement**.

Question:	Háágóó **díníyá**?	- Where are you (1) going?
Answer:	Ólta'góó **déyá**.	- I am going to the school.

Question:	John háágóó **deeyá**?	- Where is John going?
Answer:	John sodizin bá hooghangóó **deeyá**.	- John is going to the church.

Question:	Háísh béeso bá hooghangóó **deeyá**.	- Who is going to the bank?
Answer:	Mary béeso bá hooghangóó **deeyá**.	- Mary is going to the bank.

Question:	Háísha' doo hooghangóó **deeyá**a da?	- Who is not going home?
Answer:	Lee doo hooghangóó **deeyá**a da.	- Lee is not going home.

Other possible substitutions:
a. da'adání   - cafeteria
b. hooghan   - home
c. naaltsoos bá hooghan   - bookstore
d. da'iigis bá hooghan   - laundromat (house for washing)
e. naalyéhé bá hooghan   - trading post, general merchandise store

■ PRACTICE

Translate and answer the following questions.

1. Where are you (2) going?
Question: _____

Answer: _____

2. Where is Henry going?
Question: _____

Answer: _____

3. Who is going to the trading post?
Question: _____

Answer: _____

4. Where are they (3+) going?
Question: _____

Answer: _____

5. Who is not going to the laundromat?
Question: _____

Answer: _____

COMMON PHRASES

The following common phrases are useful in talking about going somewhere.

Ha'át'íísh baa naniná?	- What are you doing.
Doo baa naasháhá da.	- I am not doing anything.
Diné bizaad yínishta'.	- I am studying Navajo.
Tsxį́į́łgo	- Hurry!
Áłtsé!	- Wait!
Tį́'!	- Let's go!

PATTERN - TIREDNESS

Try to discover the meaning of the sentence below in which *ch'ééh* (in vain) precedes the verb.

Ch'ééh déyá.	- I'm tired.
Ch'ééh deet'áázh	- We (2) are tired.
Mary ch'ééh deeyá nahalin.	- Mary looks tired.

As you can see, when ch'ééh precedes the verb, the combination means to be tired.

> To express tiredness, place ch'ééh before the verb deeyá.

PRACTICE

Translate the following phrases.

1. I am tired
2. He is not tired.

3. Are you (1) tired?
4. They (3+) look like they are tired.

PATTERN - TO BE FROM

Another GO VERB that is very useful is TO BE WALKING AROUND found on page 126 in the Conversational Navajo Dictionary. It is used in patterns such as TO BE DOING, TO BE AT, and TO BE FROM. In this lesson we will learn how to be from one's hometown using the verb TO BE WALKING AROUND.

	SINGULAR	DUAL	PLURAL
1ST PERSON	naashá	neiit'aash	neiikai
2ND PERSON	naniná	naah'aash	naahkai
3RD PERSON	naaghá	naa'aash	naakai

Note: Unlike most verbs, GO VERBS are conjugated in both the 3rd person singular and dual forms.

In the patterns demonstrated below, notice that the <u>answer</u> replaces the <u>interrogative</u>. Observe also the **subject-verb agreement**.

        Question: <u>Háádéé'</u> **naniná?**   - Where are you from?
        Answer: <u>Phoenixdéé'</u> **naashá**   - I am from Phoenix.

        Question: Albuquerquedéé' **nanináásh?**   - Are you from Albuquerque?
        Answer: Aoo', Albuquerquedéé' **naashá.**   - Yes, I am from Albuquerque.

        Question: <u>Háísh</u> Shiprockdéé' **naaghá?**   - Who is from Shiprock?
        Answer: <u>Lucy</u> Shiprockdéé' **naaghá.**   - Lucy is from Shiprock.

■   PRACTICE

Translate and answer the following questions.

1. Where are you from?
Question: _____

Answer: _____

2. Where is the leader from?
Question: _____

Answer: _____

3. Where are you (2) from?
Question: _____

Answer: _____

4. Who is from Phoenix?
Question: _____

Answer: _____

5. Are you (1) from Flagstaff?
Question: _____

Positive Answer: _____

Negative Answer: _____

6. Where are they (3+) from?
Question: _____

Answer: _____

LESSON 5 DIRECTION AND PLACE

VOCABULARY

-di	- at	nihi-	-ours
háadi	- where at?	nihi-	- yours (plural)
ko-	- here	a-	- someone's
ńléí	- over there	béeso	- money
áá-	- there far	ch'iyáán	- food
aa-	- there near	éé'	- clothes (bi'éé' - his clothes)
shi-	- my	ké	- shoes (bikee' - her shoes)
ni-	- your (singular)	baghan	- his home
bi-	- his/hers	naaltsoos	- book

■ PRACTICE

Practice the vocabulary words outloud until you can recite them from memory.

■ PATTERN - PREFIXES AND SUFFIXES SHOWING DIRECTION OR PLACE

In the previous lessons, we learned two interrogatives: *háágóó* (where to?) and *háádéé'* (where from?). Another interrogative that follows the same question-answer pattern is *háadi* (*sh, shạ'*) meaning where at? *Háadi* is composed of the the interrogative *háá* (where?) and the suffix *di* (at).

Háadi can be used to describe where something is at or where someone is at in combination with the verb naaghá.

> The following prefixes can be combined with the suffixes -*góó* (to), -*déé'* (from), and -*di* (at):
>
> | | |
> |---|---|
> | ko- | - here |
> | ńléí- | - over there |
> | áá- | - there far |
> | aa- | - there near |

Examples:	Ńléígóó déyá.	- I am going (to) over there.
	Kodi naaghá.	- He is (at) here.
	Áadi naakai.	- They (3+) are (at) there far.
	Aadi naa'aash.	- They (2) are (at) there near.

51

PRACTICE

Answer the following questions using the prefixes of *ko-*, *ńléí-*, *áá-*, *aa-*, or a specific place in combination with the suffix *-di.*. In your answer, be sure to have the subject and verb agree.

0. Question: John <u>háadi</u> naaghá?
   Answer: John <u>kodi</u> naaghá.

1. Question: Mary dóó Helen háadi naa'aash?
   Answer: _____.

2. Question: Háíshạ' ńléidi naaghá?
   Answer: _____.

3. Question: Háadi naah'aash?
   Answer: _____.

4. Question: Markísh áadi naaghá?
   Answer: _____.

5. Question: Háísh aadi naakai?
   Answer: _____.

POSSESSIVE ADJECTIVES

Look at the underlined words the the following phrases:

<u>my</u> book   <u>your</u> food   <u>her</u> money   <u>his</u> clothes

Words like those underlined above come before nouns to show ownership or possession. They are called <u>possessive adjectives</u>. Now look at how possesion is shown in Navajo phrases.

<u>shi</u>naaltsoos   <u>ni</u>ch'iyáán   <u>bi</u>béeso   <u>bi</u>'éé'

Notice that ownership or possession in Navajo is also shown be <u>possessive adjectives</u>. Possessive adjectives in Navajo are just personal pronouns whose tone has changed from high to low. Also, instead of being separate words (as they are in English), they are attached directly to the noun. Look at some irregular words.

ké	- shoes	hooghan	- home
bikee'	- his shoes	baghan	- her home

52

Sometimes the noun changes when it is possessed. The Conversational Navajo Dictionary indicates this change by putting the possessed form of the noun in parentheses. Now look at the words below.

shimá	- my mother	nigod	- your knee
amá	- a mother (someone's)	agod	- a knee (someone's)

Nouns that are the names of body parts or family relationships (hand, foot, mother, son etc.) always must be combined with a possesive adjective. If the possessive adjective is not in 1st, 2nd, or 3rd person, use the indefinite possessive adjective *a-*.

> Possession is shown by attaching a possesive adjective
> (a low-toned personal pronoun) to a noun.

■ PRACTICE

Form the indicated possessive adjectives and attach them to the nouns below.

1. *my* naat'áanii _____

2. *your (1)* naaltsoos _____

3. *your (3+)* éé' _____

4. *his* béeso _____

5. *their (2)* ké _____

6. *her* ch'iyáán _____

7. *our (2)* hooghan _____

8. *my* naaltsoos _____

9. *our (2)* béeso _____

10. *your (2)* ké _____

Note: The possessed form of hooghan can also be used refer to a person's place of residence.

Examples:

| Question: Háadishą' naghan? | - Where is your home (where do you live?) |
| Answer: Shiprockdi shaghan. | - My home is at Shiprock (I live at Shiprock). |

In this example, the noun hooghan acts like a verb. While there are other verbs which specifically mean TO RESIDE, such as *kééhasht'į* - I reside see page 102 Conversational Navajo Dictionary, this noun/verb is also commonly used.

53

LESSON 6   STATE-OF-BEING VERBS

VOCABULARY

yá'át'ééh	- it is good
hóló̜	- it exists
ádin	- it is absent
át'é	- it is
nahalin	- it resembles it
amá (bimá)	- mother (his mother)
azhé'é (bizhé'é)	- father (his father)
dóó	- and
chidí	- car
tó	- water
na'ídíkid	- question
ńt'ę́ę́'	- it was, used to be
dooleeł (doo)	- it will be

■   PRACTICE

Practice the vocabulary words outloud until you can recite them from memory.

GRAMMAR

■   ACTION AND STATE-OF-BEING VERBS

Verbs in Navajo are either action verbs or state-of-being verbs*. An action verb describes an action, such as the following:

naaghá	- he is walking around
déyá	- I am going
íyą́	- you are eating
diit'ash	- we will go

A state-of-being verb, in contrast, describes a quality (such as being heavy or orange) or a state of being (such as sitting or standing). There is no reference to any preceding time or action.

nihidziil	- we are strong
bóhólnííh	- she is in charge
nahalin	- it resembles it

* In other reference texts, action verbs are called "active" and state-of-being verbs are called "neuter".

54

STATE-OF-BEING VERBS

Next we will learn five state-of-being verbs in their third person forms. The first and second person forms of these verbs are less frequently used. For example, people don't often say yá'ánisht'ééh - I am good or yá'ániit'ééh - we are good. You should remember, however, that each of these verbs can be conjugated for all three persons.

yá'át'ééh	- it is good/they (2) are good.
yá'ádaat'ééh	- they (3+) are good.

Examples:

Naaltsoos yá'át'ééh.	- The book is good.
Nihichidí yá'ádaat'ééh	- Your cars are good.

hóló̜	- it exists/they (2) exist
dahóló̜	- they (3+) exist

Examples:

Shimá dóó shizhé'é hóló̜.	- I have a mother and father. (My mother and father exist.)
Bichidí dahóló̜.	- Their cars exist. (They have cars.)

ádin	- it is absent, gone/they (2) are absent, gone
ádaadin	- they (3+) are absent, gone

Examples:

Shina'ídíkid ádin.	- I don't have a question. (My question is absent.)
Nihi'éé' ádaadin.	- We don't have any clothes. (Our clothes are absent.)

át'é	- it is/they (2) are
ádaat'é	- they (3+) are

Examples:

Tó át'é.	- It is water.
Chidí ádaat'é.	- They are cars.

nahalin	- it/they (2) resemble it
ndahalin	- they (3+) resemble it

Examples:

Shimá nimá nahalin.	- My mother resembles your mother.
Bi̜i̜h jádí ndahalin.	- Deer resemble antelope.

DESCRIBING FUTURE AND PAST STATES OF BEING

State-of-being verbs describe a condition without reference to its time - whether in the past or in the future. In order to describe a past or future condition, additional helper words must be used. Discover what these words are from the following examples.

Examples:

Yá'át'ééh.	- It <u>is</u> good.
Yá'át'ééh <u>ńt'ę́ę́'</u>.	- It <u>was</u> good.
Yá'át'ééh <u>dooleeł</u>.	- It <u>will be</u> good.

Shibéeso át'é.	- It <u>is</u> my money.
Shibéeso át'éé <u>ńt'ę́ę́'</u>.	- It <u>was</u> my money. (notice the lengthening of the é on át'é.)
Shibéeso át'ee <u>dooleeł</u>.	- It <u>will be</u> my money. (notice the lengthening and rounding down of the é on át'é.)

Notice that when *ńt'ę́ę́'* (it was, used to be) follows a state-of-being verb, the combination describes a past state of being. The combination of a state-of-being verb and *dooleeł* (it will become) describes a future state of being. It should also be noted that often *ńt'ę́ę́'* is pronounced and written *ńt'éé'*, without the nasal tone on the vowels; *dooleeł* is often shortened to *doo*. The lengthening and/or rounding down of the final vowel is for ease of pronuciation.

State-of-being verb + *ńt'ę́ę́'* describes a past condition

State-of-being verb + *dooleeł* describes a future condition

■ PRACTICE

Translate the following sentences, then describe them as past and future states of being by using *ńt'ę́ę́'* and *dooleeł*.

1. The books (3+) are good.

Translate: _____

Past: _____

Future: _____

2. My money exists.

Translate: _____

Past: _____

Future: _____

3. Our food is gone.

Translate: _____

Past: _____

Future: _____

4. They are her clothes.

Translate: _____

Past: _____

Future: _____

5. Your car resembles my car.

Translate: _____

Past: _____

Future: _____

6. My question exists (I have a question).

Translate: _____

Past: _____

Future: _____

7. Your (1) car is good.

Translate: _____

Past: _____

Future: _____

8. His books are gone.

Translate: _____

Past: _____

Future: _____

9. Whose shoe is it?

Translate: _____

Past: _____

Future: _____

10. Your (1) clothes look like her clothes.

Translate: _____

Past: _____

Future: _____

11. What is it?

Translate: _____

Past: _____

Future: _____

LESSON 7 POSTPOSITION-VERB COMBINATIONS

VOCABULARY

dibé	- sheep	bééhózin	- it is known
tł'ízí	- goat	hózhǫ́	- there is happiness
mósí	- cat	nantł'ah	- it is difficult
łééchąą'í	- dog	bił yá'át'ééh	- she likes it
bilééchąą'í	- his dog	bił bééhózin	- he knows it
bił	- with him	bił nantł'ah	- it is difficult for him
bich'į'	- to him; toward him	bił hózhǫ́	- she is happy
baa	- about it; to her	bee hólǫ́	- he has it
bee	- by means of it; concerning it	bee ádin	- he doesn't have it
		naanish	- work
déíji'éé'	- shirt; blouse		
tł'aaji'éé'	- pants		
éé'tsoh	- coat		

■ PRACTICE

Practice the vocabulary words above until you can recite them from memory.

GRAMMAR

In the Grammar Preview lesson, we learned that postpositional phrases in Navajo are used to express the same ideas as prepositional phrases do in English. We will first learn about forming postpositional phrases with pronouns as objects. Look at the words below.

        shí + ił-----------------------> shił
        me + with--------------------> me-with

        ni + ch'į' ----------------------> nich'į'
        you + to ---------------------> you-to

Notice that in English prepositional phrases. the preposition and the pronoun object are two separate words (for example, "with me"). However, in Navajo the pronoun is attached to the postposition to form one word. For example, the pronoun shí (me) is attached to the postposition -ił (with) to form the single word shił (me-with). The pronoun tells "who" and the postposition tells "what". You may have also noticed that the high tone is dropped on the pronoun. Now look at the following postpositional phrases.

        bi + aa ----------------------> baa
        her + about -----------------> her-about

58

nihi + ee ------------> nihee
us + concerning ---> us-concerning

Notice that in these combinations, the final "i" of the pronoun is dropped. This is a common sound change that occurs when pronouns are combined with postpositions. Look below at how postpositions are listed in the Conversational Navajo Dictionary and in this text.

ABOUT IT, TO HIM - baa   CONCERNING IT - bee
TOWARD HIM - bich'į'   WITH HIM - bił

Each of the above postpositions are listed with the third person *bi* (him, her, it) attached to it. Now see how this changes to indicate different persons.

shił	me-with
nił	you-with
bił	him-with
nihił	us-with
nihił	you (2+)-with

To change a postpositional phrase to indicate different persons, the pronoun for that person is substituted for *bi*.

> In a postpositional phrase with a pronoun as the object,
> the pronoun is attached directly to the postposition.

■ PRACTICE

A. The first postposition in each set is attached to the third-person pronoun *bi*. Change the pronouns in the blanks to indicate the person listed.

1.   bich'į' (to him)

   1st singular _____   1st dual _____

   2nd singular _____   2nd dual _____

2.   baa   (about him)

   1st singular _____   1st dual _____

   2nd singular _____   2nd dual _____

3.   bee   (by means of it, concerning it)

   1st singular _____   1st dual _____

   2nd singular _____   2nd dual _____

B.   Translate the following postpositional phrases:

1.   about me   _____

2.   toward you (1) _____

3.   with us   _____

4.   about you (2)   _____

5.   by means of them _____

6.   concerning me   _____

7.   with you (1)   _____

8.   toward me   _____

9.   about him   _____

10.   about you (1)   _____

■   POSTPOSITIONAL PHRASES WITH NOUNS

In English prepositional phrases, the noun follows the preposition.

Examples: with George   to the leader   concerning Navajo

Now look at the equivalent Navajo postpositional phrases with nouns as objects.

Examples: George bił   naat'áanii bich'į'   diné bizaad bee

Notice that the noun precedes the postposition. Also notice that the pronoun *bi* is attached to the postposition even though the object of the postposition is a noun. The pronoun *bi* is there to indicate that the postposition's object is in third person (remember that all nouns are in the third person).

> In a postpositional phrase with a noun as the object, the pronoun *bi* is attached to the postposition and the noun precedes this combination.

■   PRACTICE

Translate the following postpositional phrases with nouns.

1.   with Mary   _____

2.   about Henry   _____

3.   concerning the man _____

4.   toward the woman _____

POSTPOSITION - VERB COMBINATIONS

Compare the following English sentences.

> It tastes good to me.
> It tastes good to you.
> It tastes good to her.
> It tastes good to us.

Notice that the verb in these sentences is "tastes," the third-person form of "to taste". In each sentence the verbs stays the same, but the pronoun of the prepositonal phrase "to ___" changes to give the sentence a different meaning. A similar thing happens in Navajo sentences that use a postposition-verb combination. Note: this postposition-verb combination does <u>not</u> mean to "taste good", it refers rather to like something.

Shił yá'át'ééh	It is good with me (I like it).
Nił yá'át'ééh	It is good with you (You like it).
Bił yá'át'ééh	It is good with him (He likes it).
Nihił yá'át'ééh	It is good with us (2) (We like it).
Nihił yá'át'ééh	It is good with you (2) (You 2 like it).

As you can see, the third person verb form yá'át'ééh stays the same in each sentence. The pronoun of the postpositional phrase changes to give the sentence a different meaning each time. -ił yá'át'ééh ("it is good with ___") is called a <u>posposition-verb combination</u>. Postposition-verb combinations are conjugated by changing the pronoun profixed to the postposition. Here are some examples of how they are used in larger sentences.

Naaltsoos shił yá'át'ééh.	I like books.
Béeso nił yá'át'ééh.	You like money.
Mósí bił yá'át'ééh.	She likes cats.
Ólta' doo nihił yá'át'ééh da.	We (2) don't like school.
Shichidí doo nihił yá'át'ééh da.	You don't like my car.

You will find postposition-verb combinations listed in the Conversational Navajo Dictionary with the third person pronoun *bí* attached to the postposition. There are oodles of them; they are listed as (postp-vb). Below are some very useful postposition-verb combinations.

Bił yá'át'ééh.	With him it is good (He likes it).
Bił nantł'ah.	With him it is difficult (It is difficult for him).
Bił bééhózin	With her it is known (She knows it).
Bił hózhǫ́	With her there is happiness (She is happy).
Bee hólǫ	Concerning him it exists (He has it).
Bee ádin	Concerning her it is absent (She doesn't have it).

61

■ PRACTICE

1. Practice conjugating each of the preceding postposition-verb combinations through 1st, 2nd, and 3rd persons until you can do them fluently.

2. Answer the following questions.
    0. Béesoósh nee hóló?
    Answer: <u>Aoo' béeso shee hóló'.</u>

    1. Chidísh nee hóló?
    Answer: _____

    2. Naaltsoosísh nił yá'át'ééh?
    Answer: _____

    3. Diné bizaad nił nantł'ahísh?
    Answer: _____

    4. Háísh déíji'éé' bee ádin?
    Answer: _____

    5. Ha'át'íísh nił bééhózin?
    Answer: _____

    6. Háísh tł'aaji'éé' bee hóló?
    Answer: _____

    7. Ha'át'íísh doo nił yá'át'ééh da?
    Answer: _____

    8. Háíshą' doo bił hózhóó da?
    Answer: _____

    9. **Éé'tsoh nee hólónísh?**
    Answer: _____

    10. Ha'át'íísh nił nantł'ah?
    Answer: _____

    11. Háísh dibé bee hóló?
    Answer: _____

    12. Ha'át'íísh doo nił bééhózin da?
    Answer: _____

    13. K'adísh nił hózhó?
    Answer: _____

PLURAL FORMS OF POSTPOSITION-VERB COMBINATIONS

So far we have learned how to conjugate postposition-verb combinations in their singular and dual forms only. We will now learn to conjugate them in their plural forms. Look at the example below to see how this is done.

	SINGULAR	DUAL	PLURAL
1ST PERSON	shee hółǫ́	nihee hółǫ́	nihee dahółǫ́
2ND PERSON	nee hółǫ́	nihee hółǫ́	nihee dahółǫ́
3RD PERSON		bee hółǫ́	bee dahółǫ́

Notice that a postposition-verb combination is conjugated in its plural form simply by replacing the singular/dual form of the verb with the plural form. Below are the plural forms of the verbs in this lesson:

Singular/Dual	Plural
hółǫ́	dahółǫ́
ádin	ádaadin
yá'át'ééh	yá'ádaat'ééh
nantł'ah	ndantł'ah
hózhǫ́	dahózhǫ́
bééhózin	béédahózin

You're probably wondering why the "*da*" plural marker sometimes in front of the verb, and sometimes it is inside the verb. Good question. Hundreds of years ago someone knew that you would be trying to learn this and purposely made it more difficult just for you! Not really. Remember in the Grammar Preview lesson we briefly discussed morpheme position. The plural marker is always in position # 3. When the "*da*" plural marker is inside the verb, it means that there are already morphemes in position #1 or #2; when the "*da*" plural marker is in in the initial position, it means that there are no morphemes in position #1 or #2.

> To form a plural postposition-verb combination, replace the singular/dual form of the verb with the plural form.

Examples:

Diné bizaad nihił bééhózin.
We (2) know Navajo.

Diné bizaad nihił béédahózin.
We (3+) know Navajo.

Ólta' nihił nantł'ah.
School is hard for us (2).

Ólta' nihił ndantł'ah.
School is hard for us (3+).

PRACTICE

A. Change each of the following postposition-verb combinations to its plural form.

Dual   Plural

1. nihee hóló̧   _____

2. bee ádin   _____

3. nihił yá'át'ééh _____

4. bił hózhǫ́   _____

5. nihił nantł'ah   _____

6. nihił bééhózin   _____

B. Answer the following questions.

Example:

0.   Ha'át'íísh doo nihił yá'ádaat'ééh da?

Answer: Naanish doo nihił yá'ádaat'ééh da.

1.   Ha'át'íísh nihee dahóló̧?

Answer: _____

2.   Chidíísh nihee dahóló̧?

Answer: _____

3.   Diné bizaad nihił ndantł'ahísh?

Answer: _____

4.   Ólta'ísh nihił yá'ádaat'ééh?

Answer: _____

5.   Háíshą' doo bił dahózhǫǫ da?

Answer: _____

6.   Ha'át'íísh nihił béédahózin?

Answer: _____

64

LESSON 8   MORE POSTPOSITION-VERB COMBINATIONS

VOCABULARY

ałdó'	- also; too
-dó'	- also; too
shidó'	- me too
háidí (sh,shą')	- which one?
díí	- this
eii	- that; those near
éí	- that; those farther away
ńléí	- that over there; those over there
adinídíín	- light
bé'ézhóó'	- comb
tsésǫ'	- window
dáádílkał	- door
nizhóní	- it is pretty, beautiful
bił nizhóní	- she thinks it is pretty; she likes it
deesdoi	- it is hot (weather)
bił deesdoi	- he is hot
hoolzhiizh	- a time has come
baa hoolzhiizh	- it is her turn
bił hóyéé'	- he is lazy
bich'į' nahwii'ná	- he is having problems

▪ PRACTICE

Practice the vocabulary words above until you can recite them from memory.

GRAMMAR

▪ *-shą'* and *ya'* QUESTION MARKERS

We have already learned the question marker *-ísh (sh)*. Try to discover two more question markers in the following sentences below.

Tłízí át'é.	- It is a goat.
Tłízí át'é, ya'?	- It is a goat, right?
Aoo' tłízí át'é.	- Yes, it is a goat.
Nihił dahózhǫ́.	- You (3+) are happy.
Nihił dahózhǫ́, ya'	- You (3+) are happy, huh?
Ndaga' doo nihił dahózhǫ́ǫ da.	- No, we (3+) are not happy.

65

Ya' is a question marker that follows a sentence or phrase. It is equivalent to "_____, right?" or "_____, huh?" Notice that *ya'* requires a yes or no answer just like the *-ísh* question marker does.

Look for another question marker in the sentences below.

Chidí shee hólǫ. Nishą'?	- I have a car. What about you?
Shidó'. Chidí shee hólǫ.	- Me too. I have a car.
Diné bizaad shił nantł'ah. Nishą'?	- Navajo is difficult for me. How about you?
Shí doo Diné bizaad shił nantł'ah da.	- Navajo is not difficult for me.

Notice that the question marker *-shą'* attaches the the end of a word (usually a noun, pronoun, interrogative). It is equivalent to "What about_____?" or "How about_____?". *-Shą'* is not a yes-no question and should be answered with an explanation.

QUESTION MARKER	WHERE ATTACHED	MEANING
ya'	end of sentence	"_____, right? "_____, huh?
-shą'	end of noun, pronoun or interrogative	"How about_____?" "What about_____?"

DEMONSTRATIVES

In English, "this," "that," and "that over there" are used to point out objects and persons. They are called demonstratives because the "demonstrate" or point out what is being referred to.

In Navajo, as in English, the demonstrative used depends upon the location of the object in relation to the speaker and the person being spoken to. Some of the demonstratives in Navajo are listed below.

díí	- this; these
eii	- that; those (nearby)
éí	- that; those (more distant)
ńléí	- that over there; those over there

As you can see, *díí, eii, éí,* and *ńléí* can refer to more than one object or person. Demonstratives are generally used at the beginning of a sentence or phrase.

Examples:

Díí ha'át'íísh át'é?	- What is this?
Eii tsésǫ' át'é.	- That is a window.
Éí adínídíín ádaat'é.	- Those are lights.
Ńléí tł'ízí ndahalin.	- Those over there look like goats.
Díí éé'tsoh nizhóní.	- This coat is pretty.
Éí chidí shił yá'át'ééh.	- I like that car.
Dííshą'	- How about this one?

A common interrogative used with the demonstratives listed above is Háidí - which one? Notice how it is used the in the questions below.

Question:	Háidí nił yá'át'ééh?	- Which one do you like?
Answer:	Díí shił yá'át'ééh.	- I like this.
Question:	Háidí ninaaltsoos át'é?	- Which one is your book?
Answer:	Eii shinaaltsoos át'é.	- That is my book.

In combination with the demonstratives above, the suffix *-dí* can be added to refer to a specific item. Notice how it adds specificity to the sentences below.

Question:	Háidí nił yá'át'ééh?	- Which one do you like?
Answer:	Díidí shił yá'át'ééh.	- I like this <u>specific one</u>.
Question:	Háidí ninaaltsoos át'é?	- Which one is your book?
Answer:	Eiidí shinaaltsoos át'é.	- That <u>specific one</u> is my book.

■ PRACTICE

Answer the following questions. Remember that often when the question is posed with *díí* (this), the reply uses *eii.* (that) and vice versa.

0. Question: <u>Díí</u> ha'át'íísh át'é?   - What is <u>this</u>?
   Answer: <u>Eii</u> dibé át'é.   - <u>That</u> is a sheep.

1. Question: Eii ha'át'íísh át'é? (pointing to a window)
   Answer: _____

2. Question: Díí háísh bibéeso át'ée dooleeł?
   Answer: _____

3. Question: Ńléí at'ééd nizhóní, ya'?
   Answer: _____

4. Question: Éí dibé tł'ízí nahalinísh?
   Answer: _____

67

5. Question: Háidí chidí ayóó nił yá'át'ééh?
   Answer: _____

6. Question: Eii háísh bilééchąą'í át'é?
   Answer: _____

7. Question: Niísh ałdó' łééchąą'í nee hólǫ́?
   Answer: _____

8. Question: Diné bizaad shił nantł'ah. Nishą'?
   Answer: _____

9. Question: Háidí tł'aaji'éé' doo nizhóní da.
   Answer: _____

10. Question: Díí nidéíji'éé' át'é, ya'?
    Answer: _____

■ PATTERNS - MORE POSTPOSITION-VERB COMBINATIONS

Following are five more postposition-verb combinations. The plural form of the verb is in parentheses.

bił nizhóní (danizhóní)	- she likes it; she thinks it is pretty
bił deesdoi (dadeesdoi)	- he is hot
bił hóyéé' (dahóyéé')	- she is lazy
baa hoolzhiizh (dahoolzhiizh)	- it is his turn
bich'į' nahwii'ná (ndahwii'ná)	- she is having troubles, problems

Examples:

Díí éé'tsoh shił nizhóní.	- I like this coat (think it is pretty).
Ayóó shił deesdoi.	- I am very hot.
Ńléí ashkii bił hóyéé'.	- That boy over there is lazy.
K'ad, háísh baa hoolzhiizh?	- Now. whose turn is it?
Shich'į' nahwii'náá ńt'ę́ę́'	- I used to have problems.

■ PRACTICE

1. Practice conjugating the five postposition-verb combinations above until you can recite them fluently.

2. Translate and answer the following questions. In your answers utilize the demonstratives, intensifiers, and past and future markers when present in the question.

68

1. Who is lazy?
Question: _____
Answer: _____

2. Are you (3+) hot?
Question: _____
Answer: _____

3. Now, whose turn is it?
Question: _____
Answer: _____

4. Who didn't have problems (in the past).
Question: _____
Answer: _____

5. Do you (1) like (think it's pretty) my blouse?
Question: _____
Answer: _____

6. Which book did you (1) like?
Question: _____
Answer: _____

7. Whose money will this be?
Question: _____
Answer: _____

8. What will you (3+) know?
Question: _____
Answer: _____

9. Is that (near) your cat?
Question: _____
Answer: _____

10. Whose home is that over there?
Question: _____
Answer: _____

LESSON 9   NUMBERS AND TIME

VOCABULARY

dikwíí (sh, shạ')	- how many?	-ts'áadah	- teen
oolkił	- it is passing (time)	-diin	- ty
-di	- times	jį́	- day
ałníí'	- half	dóó ałníí'	- and half
ba'aan	- in addition to it	ha'íí'ą́ągo	- sunrise
t'ááłá'í	- one	abínígo	- morning
naaki	- two	dé'oo'ááł	- midmorning
táá'	- three	ałní'ní'ą́	- noon
dį́į'	- four	hííłch'ị'go	- afternoon
ashdla'	- five	yaa ádeez'ą́ągo	- late afternoon
hastą́ą́	- six	i'íí'ą́ągo	- sundown
tsosts'id	- seven	tł'éé'go	- at night
tseebíí	- eight	tł'éé' ałníí'	- midnight
náhást'éí	- nine	nááhai	- years
neeznáá	- ten		

■   PRACTICE

Practice the above vocabulary words until you can recite them from memory.

■   NUMBERS

The numbers from one to ten are:

t'ááłá'í	- one	hastą́ą́	- six
naaki	- two	tsosts'id	- seven
táá'	- three	tseebíí	- eight
dį́į'	- four	náhást'éí	- nine
ashdla'	- five	neeznáá	- ten

The suffix -ts'áadah is the Navajo equivalent of the English "-teen". The numbers between ten and twenty are combinations of the numbers one through nine and the suffix -ts'áadah (except for fifteen and sixteen, which drop the "ts").

ła'ts'áadah	- eleven	hastą́'áadah	- sixteen
naakits'áadah	- twelve	tsosts'idts'áadah	- seventeen
táá'ts'áadah	- thirteen	tseebííts'áadah	- eighteen
dį́į'ts'áadah	- fourteen	náhást'éíts'áadah	- nineteen
ashdla' áadah	- fifteen		

70

Just as there are a few sound changes in English in the teen numbers (three + teen -->thirteen and five + teen -->fifteen), you probably noticed a few sound changes in Navajo as well. At least in Navajo the teen numbers start with eleven instead of the arbitrary thirteen as in English. Just think of it, an eleven year-old teenager!

The suffix -*diin* is the equivalent of the English "-ty". The multiples of ten from twenty to one hundred are the combination of the numbers from one through ten and the suffix -*diin*. Again there are a few sound changes that occur for ease of pronunciation.

naadiin	- twenty	tsosts'idiin	- seventy
tádiin	- thirty	tseebíídiin	- eighty
dízdiin	- forty	náhást'éídiin	- ninety
ashdladiin	- fifty	neeznádiin	- tenty (one hundred)
hastą́diin	- sixty		

In English, we say "twenty-one," "twenty-two," etc.. The same process is used for numbers between twenty and thirty in Navajo. You combine *naadiin* with one of the numbers from one to nine.

naadiin ła'	- twenty-one	naadiin hastą́ą́	- twenty-six
naadiin naaki	- twenty-two	naadiin tsosts'id	- twenty-seven
naadiin táá'	- twenty-three	naadiin tseebíí	- twenty-eight
naadiin dį́į́'	- twenty-four	naadiin náhást'éí	- twenty-nine
naadiin ashdla'	- twenty-five		

Note: Sometimes the final "n" in naadiin is dropped as a sound change. Example: naadįła', naadįnaaki. Notice that the nasalized sound remains on the įį.

For numbers past thirty, *dóó ba'aan* (in addition to it) is inserted between the numbers. In other words, numbers are expressed in expanded notation. In English were somewhat spoiled by taking shorcuts in expressing numbers; for both $19.99 and 1,999 we say "nineteen ninety-nine", when we really mean nineteen dollars and ninety-nine cents or one thousand nine hundred and ninety-nine. Navajo doesn't have any short cuts for numbers, yet.

Examples:

tádiin dóó ba'aan t'ááłá'í	- thirty-one
ashdladiin dóó ba'aan tsosts'id	- fifty-seven
tsosts'idiin dóó ba'aan naaki	- seventy-two
tseebíídiin dóó ba'aan dį́į́'	- eighty-four

For multiples of one hundred, the suffix -*di* (times) is added to neeznádiin.

Examples:

naakidi neeznádiin	- two hundred
táá'di neeznádiin	- three hundred
dį́į́'di neeznádiin	- four hundred
ashdladi neeznádiin dóó ba'aan dízdiin dóó ba'aan tsosts'id	- five hundred forty-seven
náhástéídi neeznádiin dóó ba'aan tseebíídiin dóó ba'aan naaki	- nine hundred eight-two

In Navajo, one thousand is *mííl*, after the Spanish *mil*. In English we use the <u>mil</u> for a thousand as well. In metric measurement, think of a <u>milli</u>meter, one thousandth of a meter. Medicine is often dispensed in ml or <u>milli</u>liters.

T'ááłá'ídi mííl dóó ba'aan náhást'éídi neeznádiin dóó ba'aan náhástéídiin dóó ba'aan ashdla' (1995 - the year this text was written) I hope you don't live that long, because next we're going to learn how to tell age.

■ PRACTICE

Write out and say the following numbers.

1. six _____ _____

2. fifteen _____

3. twenty-four _____

4. forty-three _____

5. seventy-eight _____

6. ninety-nine _____

7. one hundred fifty-two _____

8. six hundred and thirty-one _____

9. This year _____

10. The year you were born _____

■ PATTERNS - TELLING YOUR AGE

The patterns below are used to talk about someone's age.

1. Question: <u>Dikwíísh</u> ninááhai?   - <u>How old</u> are you?
    Answer: <u>Number</u> shinááhai.   - I am <u>number</u> years old.

2. Question: John <u>dikwíísh</u> binááhai?   - How <u>old</u> is John?
    Answer: John <u>naadiin</u> binááhai.   - John is <u>twenty</u> years old.

3. Question: Nizhé'é <u>dikwíísh</u> binááhai?   - <u>How old</u> is your father?
    Answer: Shizhé'é <u>ashdladiin</u> binááhai. - My father is <u>fifty</u> years old.

PRACTICE

Answer the following questions.

1.   Dikwíísh nínááhai?

Answer: _____

2.   Nimá dikwíísh bínááhai?

Answer: _____

3.   Bá ólta'í dikwííshą' bínááhai?

Answer: _____

4.   Háísh dízdiin bínááhai?

Answer: _____

PATTERNS - TELLING TIME

The following patterns will help you begin telling (clock) time in Navajo.

Question: Dikwíidi oolkił?	- What time is it?
Answer: Táá'di oolkił.	- It is three o'clock.
OR	
Answer: Díí' dóó ałníí'di oolkił.	- It is four-thirty.
OR	
Answer: Ałní'ní'ą́.	- It is noon.
OR	
Answer: Tł'éé' ałníí'.	- It is midnight.

Before clocks were introduced to the Navajo people, time was generally expressed by the movement of the sun. Here are a few "time periods" that are useful.

ha'íí'ą́ągo	- sunrise
abínígo	- morning
dé'oo'ááł	- midmorning (the sun is rising across)
ałní'ní'ą́	- noon (the sun is half way across)
hííłch'į' go	- afternoon (the day and night are coming together)
yaa ádeez'ą́ągo	- late afternoon (the sun is going down)
i'íí'ą́ągo	- sundown (the sun has gone down)
tł'éé'go	- night (referring to being dark)

73

Fill in the blanks with the appropriate response to the question "*Dikwíidi oolkilʔ*"

1. Answer: _____

2. Answer: _____

3. Answer: _____

4. Answer: _____

5. Answer: _____

6. Answer: _____

7. Answer: _____

8. Answer: _____

LESSON 10 MONEY AND BUYING

VOCABULARY

łichíí'	- penny (it is red)
tsindao	- penny (from spanish centavo)
łitso	- nickel (it is yellow)
dootł'izh	- dime (it is blue/green/turquoise)
gíinsi	- fifteen cents (from spanish quince)
yááł	- bit (1/8th of a dollar)
naaki yááł	- two bits
díí' yááł	- four bits
hastą́ą́ yááł	- six bits
béeso	- dollar
nahaniih	- it is sold
ílį́	- it is valuable
bą́ą́h ílį́	- it costs
chidí bitoo'	- gasoline
táláwosh	- soap
t'éiyá	- only

■ PRACTICE

Practice the above vocabulary words until you can recite them from memory.

■ PATTERNS - MONEY

Below are the names of the various denominations of money.

łichíí'	- penny (it is red)
tsindao	- penny (from spanish centavo)
łitso	- nickel (it is yellow)
dootł'izh	- dime (it is green/blue/turquoise)
gíinsi	- fifteen cents (from spanish quince)
yááł	- bit (1/8th of a dollar, from spanish real-pronounce reyááł)
naaki yááł	- two bits $.25
díí yááł	- four bits $.50
hastą́ą́ yááł	- six bits $.75
béeso	- dollar (from spanish peso)

The Navajo system of money originally was borrowed from the Spanish from Mexico. Notice the borrowed words of tsindao (centavo), béeso (peso), and the yááł ("pieces of eight" or "bits of eight"). During the 1860's the U.S. federal government issued paper money instead of coins for a dime and nickel. A "green bill" was worth a dime; a "yellow bill" was worth a nickel.

Here are some examples of how money is counted.

Naaki béeso dóó ba'aan táá' dootł'izh t'éiyá shee hóló.
- I only have $2.30.

Díí' yáál dóó ba'aan ła' łitso nihee hóló.
- We have fifty-five cents.

■ PRACTICE

Write out and say the following amounts of money.

1. three cents _____

2. five dollars _____

3. two dimes _____

4. sixty-five cents _____

5. one dollar and seventy-five cents _____

6. ten dollars and fifty cents _____

7. twenty-five dollars _____

8. one hundred and ninety-nine dollars _____

9. fifteen cents _____

10. eighty nine cents _____

■ PATTERNS - SHOPPING

The patterns below will help you talk about shopping.

1.   Háadishą' _____ nahaniih?
       a. ch'iyáán
       b. táláwosh

- Where do they sell _____?
       a. food
       b. soap

2.   _____ dikwíí bą́ą́h ílį́?
       a. chidí bitoo'
       b. naaltsoos

- How much does _____ cost?
       a. gasoline
       b. the book

3.   _____ bą́ą́h ílį́.
    a. naaki yáál
    b. táá' béeso

- It costs _____.
       a. twenty-five cents
       b. three dollars

PRACTICE

Answer the following questions.

1.   Háadishạ' ké nahaniih?

Answer: _____

2.   Ké dikwíísh bạạh ílị́?

Answer: _____

3.   Háadishạ' éé' nahaniih?

Answer: _____

4.   Éé' dikwíí bạạh ílị́?

Answer: _____

5.   Háadi ch'iyáán nahaniih?

Answer: _____

6.   Chidí bitoo' dikwíísh bạạh ílị́?

Answer: _____

7.   Dibé dikwíísh bạạh ílị́?

Answer: _____

8.   Háadishạ' chidí nahaniih?

Answer: _____

9.   Dikwíísh béeso nee hóló̜?

Answer: _____

10.   Nichidí dikwíísh bạạh ílị́į ńt'éẹ́'?

Answer: _____

LESSON 11   FOOD AND EATING

VOCABULARY

lá'ạạ	- fine, so it is
łikan	- it is sweet, delicious
bił łikan	- it tastes good to him (postposition-verb combination)
bááh	- bread
bááh łikaní	- cake
áshįįh	- salt
áshįįh łikan	- sugar
azeedích'íí' łibáhí	- black pepper
atoo'	- stew
atsį'	- meat
nímasii	- potatoes
abe'	- milk
abe' yistiní	- ice cream
tódilchxoshí	- soda pop
dah diníilghazh	- fry bread
mandagíiya	- butter (from Spanish mantequilla)
bilasáanaa	- apple (from spanish manzana)
alóós	- rice (from Spanish arros)
naadą́ą́'	- corn
hashk'aan	- banana (same as yucca fruit)
ch'ééh jiyáán	- watermelon

■ PATTERNS - FOODS

The patterns will help you communicate at meal times.

1. _____ nił łikanísh?   - Do you like _____?
    Aoo', _____ shił łikan.   - Yes, I like _____.
    Ndaga' _____ doo shił łikan da. - No I don't like _____.
        a. abe' yistiní   a. ice cream
        b. bááh   b. bread
        c. atsį'   c. meat
        d. nímasii   d. potatoes

2. _____ shaa ní'aah.   - Pass the <u>(one bulky object)</u> to me.
      a. áshįįh   a. salt
      b. bilasáanaa   b. apple

3. _____ shaa níkaah.   - Pass the <u>(food on a plate or in an open container)</u> to me.
      a. mandagíiya   a. butter
      b. atoo'   b. soup

78

A. Answer the following questions in both the affirmative and negative.

1.   Bááh łikaní nił łikanísh?

Positive answer: _____

Negative answer: _____

2.   Bilasáanaa nił łikanísh?

Positive answer: _____

Negative answer: _____

3.   Ha'át'íísh nił łikan?

Positive answer: _____

Negative answer: _____

4.   Atsį' dóó nímasii nił łikanísh?

Positive answer: _____

Negative answer: _____

5.   Háísh ch'ééh jiyáán doo bił łikan da?

Answer: _____

B. Translate the following phrases.

1. Pass the milk (in a glass) to me.

_____

2. Pass the potatoes (in a bowl) to me.

_____

3. Pass the apple to me.

_____

4. Pass the fry bread to me (on a plate).

_____

5. Pass the salt (in a shaker) to me.

_____

GRAMMAR

◼ HANDLE VERBS

As you may have noticed in the last PATTERNS - FOODS section, there were two different ways of expressing pass it to me, depending on the size and shape of the object. In Navajo, when expressing the idea of handling something (such as picking it up, setting it down, giving it to someone, tossing it etc.) or describing its position (sitting, falling, lying etc.) the stem reflects the size and shape of the object. These stems are referred to Classifying Stems. In the Conversational Navajo Dictionary the verbs that pertain to handling objects are called Handle Verbs. Here is a brief summary of how they are used.

The part-of-speech abbreviation (hv) stands for "handle verb prefix." The prefixes are listed in the same order as a regular verb.
Example:

1st sing., 2nd sing., 3rd sing/dual/ 1st dual

BRING IT, TO (hv) nish-, ní-, yí-/ nii-,
noh-/ danii-, danoh-, deí, (áát)

2nd dual, 1st plural, 2nd plural, 3rd plural, (future stem)

To the prefixes may be added any one of the following imperfective handle verb stems:

'aah	singular bulky, round, hard object (ball, book, etc.)
yeeh	pack, burden, or load (load of wood, water, etc.)
jááh	large number of plural objects (stones, puppies, etc.)
*jiid	anything carried by l ack (pack, baby, etc.)
*jooł	non-compact matter (hay, brush, etc.)
kaah	anything in an open vessel (food, water, etc.)
lé	slender, flexible object (rope, belt, etc.)
nííł	small number of plural objects (2 or 3 books, pens, etc.)
*teeh	singular animate object (sheep, man, etc.)
tįįh	singular slender, stiff object (ruler, branch, etc.)
tłeeh	mushy matter (mud, cement, etc.)
*tsóós	flat flexible object (paper, blanket, etc.)

*These stems require the ł classifier (position 2,); the rest take the o classifier.
Examples:

Naaltsoos nish-jááh. I am bringing books.

Tł'oh shaa ní-ł-jooł. Bring the hay to me.

Dibé nihaa yí-ł-teeh. He is bringing the sheep to us.

80

Additional foods and table items are listed in the Conversational Navajo Dictionary beginning on page 140. You might note that most utinsels such as a fork or spoon are singular, stiff objects and would use the classifying stem of tı̨ı̨h. Hence, hand me a fork would be: bíla' táá'ii shaa nítı̨ı̨h. Interestingly, hand me a knife or an axe is shaa ní'aah.

■ COMMON PHRASES

Here are some common phrases that you might find useful around the dinner table.

K'ad da'iidą́.	- Let's eat.
Dichin nishłį́.	- I'm hungry.
Dibáá' nishłį́.	- I'm thirsty.
Shá hoołʼaah.	- Make room for me.
Ha'át'íísh daadą́?	- What for dinner?
Łikan halchin.	- It smells delicious.
Ayóó łikan.	- It tastes very delicious.
Náníichaad.	- I'm full.
Ahéhee'.	- Thank you
Ayóó sidó.	- It's hot (temperature).
Ayóó dich'íí'.	- It's hot or spicy.

Notice that some of the "manners" we use in English are not necessarily *spoken* in Navajo. Sure you can say, "please pass the stew," but *please* - t'áá shǫǫdí in Navajo connotates more of a begging, beseeching please. You don't have to beg for food in Navajo. It's okay to say thank you - ahéhee' or ahéhee'ḷą́ą! Your welcome is usually expressed simply as Aoo' - yes.

Mealtimes in a traditional Navajo family are special experiences. Napkins or paper towels perhaps may not be used when eating mutton. An individual prayer of thanks may be offered at the end of the meal. No parts of the sheep or goat may be wasted. Food may be prepared in simpler traditional methods using unfamiliar ingredients. There may or may not be a dinner table. The diet may not be as varied as some are accustomed to. Enjoy.

LESSON 12 HEALTH TERMS

VOCABULARY

neezgai	- it hurts
diniih	- it aches; it is sore
agaan	- arm
ajáád	- leg
atsiits'iin	- head
atsii'	- hair
átáá'	- forehead
anáá'	- eye
ajaa'	- ear
azéé'	- mouth
áchį́į́h	- nose
awos	- shoulder
akee'	- foot
ála'	- hand
agod	- knee
awoo'	- tooth
abid	- stomach

■   PRACTICE

Practice the above vocabulary until you can recite them from memory.

■   PATTERNS

The following patterns can be used to express simple health related ideas. For more anatomical terms and health assessment phrases refer to the Health Care Appendix in the Conversational Navajo Dictionary beginning on page 146.

Question: <u>Háadi</u> neezgai?	- Where does it hurt?
Answer: <u>Shigod</u> neezgai.	- My knee hurts.
Question: <u>Háadi</u> diniih?	- Where does it ache?
Answer: <u>Shítáá'</u> diniih.	- My forehead aches.

There are a number of postposition-verbs combinations that can be used in health related situations. We have learned one already - to have a cough (dikos bidoolna'). Here are a few more that may be useful. Each is listed in the third person singular form. They can be conjugated by changing the pronoun. For more health assessment phrases see the Health Care Appendix on pages 146-149 in the Conversational Navajo Dictionary.

bił náhodééyá	- He is dizzy
bitah honeezgai	- She hurts all over
bitsą́ hodiniih	- He has diahrrea
chin baah ádin	- He is clean
t'óó baa'ih	- He is dirty
baah dahaz'ą́	- She is chronically ill
biyi' hodilid	- He has heartburn
bitah yá'áhoot'ééh	- She is feeling well
bi'niilk'ai	- He is gaining weight

■ PRACTICE

Respond to the following questions.

1.   Háadi neezgai?

Answer: _____

2.   Háíshą' bikee' diniih?

Answer: _____

3.   Niwoo'ísh diniih?

Answer: _____

4.   Níla'ísh neezgai?

Answer: _____

5.   Nijaa'ísh diniih?

Answer: _____

6.   Háísh bił náhodééyá?

Answer: _____

7.   Ashkii chin baah ádinísh?

Answer: _____

8.   Háíshą' doo bitah honeezgai da?

Answer: _____

9.   Hastiiníish biyi' hodilid?

Answer: _____

10.   Asdzą́ą́níish baah dahaz'ą́?

Answer: _____

ANSWERING NEGATIVE YES-NO QUESTIONS

Compare the questions in the sets below:

1. <u>Are</u> you studying Navajo?
2. <u>Aren't</u> you studying Navajo?

1. <u>Is</u> he going to the store?
2. <u>Isn't</u> he going to the store?

1. <u>Was</u> the movie good?
2. <u>Wasn't</u> the movie good?

The first question in each group is a <u>positive yes-no question</u>; the second question in the each group is a <u>negative yes-no question</u>. We already know how to answer positive yes-no questions in Navajo. Now we will learn how to answer negative yes-no questions.

In English, there is very little difference between negative yes-no and positive yes-no questions. Negative yes-no question are used to express some doubt, surprise, skepticism, or amazement about something. The amazing thing in English is that although the two questions are technically opposite in meaning, we answer them the same. Isn't that strange? Or should I ask, Is that strange? No matter the question. It is.

In Navajo, there is a very real difference between negative yes-no and positive yes-no questions. They are posed very literally, and as such must be answered literally. Negative yes-no questions are answered with aoo', ndaga', or dooda. <u>Aoo'</u>, while translated as "yes," means "that's right" in this case. <u>Ndaga'</u> and <u>dooda</u>, while translated as "no," mean "that's not right" in this case. Look at how they are used to answer the questions below.

Question:	Doósh nił hózhǫ́ǫ da?	- Aren't you happy?
Answer:	<u>Aoo'</u>, doo shił hózhǫ́ǫ da.	- That's right, I am not happy.
Answer:	<u>Ndaga'</u>, shił hózhǫ́.	- That's not right, I am happy.

Question:	Diné bizaad doósh nił bééhózin da?	- Don't you know Navajo?
Answer:	<u>Aoo'</u>, Diné bizaad doo shił bééhózin da.	- That's right, I don't know Navajo.
Answer:	<u>Ndaga'</u>, Diné bizaad shił bééhózin.	- That's not right, I do know Navajo.

Question:	Doósh nikee' diniih da?	- Aren't your feet sore?
Answer:	<u>Aoo'</u> shikee' doo diniih da.	- That's right, my feet are not sore.
Answer:	<u>Dooda</u>, shikee' diniih.	- That's not right, my feet are sore.

Notice that negative yes-no questions are answeredwith aoo', ndaga', or dooda, followed by an explanation.

> Negative yes-no questions are answered either by
> saying aoo' (that's right) or by saying ndaga' or
> dooda (that's not right), followed by an explanation.

■ PRACTICE

Give a positive and negative response to each question.

1.　Hashk'aan doósh niłłikan da? (Don't you like bananas?)

Positive answer: _____

Negative answer: _____

2.　Doósh ch'ééh díníyáa da? (Aren't you tired?)

Positive answer: _____

Negative answer: _____

3.　Díí chidí doósh nił nizhóní da? (Don't you think this car is nice?)

Positive answer: _____

Negative answer: _____

4.　Béeso doósh nee hólǫ́ǫ da? (Don't you have any money?)

Positive answer: _____

Negative answer: _____

5.　Naaltsoos doósh nił yá'át'ééh da? (Don't you like books?)

Positive answer: _____

Negative answer: _____

6.　K'ad doósh baa hoolzhiizh da? (Isn't it his turn now?)

Positive answer: _____

Negative answer: _____

7.　Nizhé'é doósh nahalin da? (Doesn't he look like your father?)

Positive answer: _____

Negative answer: _____

8.　Diné bizaad doósh nił bééhózin da? (Don't you know Navajo?)

Positive answer: _____

Negative answer: _____

9.　Doósh nitah yá'áhoot'ééh da? (Aren't you feeling well?)

Positive answer: _____

Negative answer: _____

LESSON 13   FAMILY RELATIONSHIPS

VOCABULARY

shimá	- my mother
shizhé'é	- my father
shicheii	- my maternal grandfather
shimásání	- my maternal grandmother
shinálí	- my paternal grandfather or grandmother
sha'áłchíní	- my children (parent speaking)
shiye'	- my son (father speaking)
shiyáázh	- my son (mother speaking)
shitsi'	- my daughter (father speaking)
shich'é'é	- daughter (mother speaking)
shádí	- my older sister
shinaaí	- my older brother
shideezhí	- my younger sister
shitsilí	- my younger brother
nishłį́	- I am
báshíshchíín	- I am born for
siláo	- police
bá'ólta'í	- teacher
hataałii	- medicine man
azee'iił'íní	- doctor
akaałii	- cowboy
dóone'é	- clan

 PRACTICE

Practice the above vocabulary words until you can recite them from memory.

GRAMMAR

   Nilį́   (He is)

Up to this point in the workbook, most of the verbs we have learned have been simple verbs (conjugated with pronouns shi-, ni-, bi-, and nihi-) or third person verb forms (which we have combined with a postposition and conjugated by changing the pronoun attached to the postposition). These two types of verbs are the easiest to learn, but they make up only a small portion of the Navajo verbs. From now on, we will primarily learn regular conjugating verbs. Several future and perfective verbs will be introduced.

The first verb we will learn is "to be," a state-of-being verb.

Nilį - He is

	SINGULAR	DUAL	PLURAL
FIRST PERSON	nishłį́	niidlį́	daniidlį́
SECOND PERSON	nílį́	nohłį́	danohłį́
THIRD PERSON		nilį́	danilį́

As you recall, we have already learned one verb that means "to be" -- the verb át'é. Át'é, when it is used with a person, refers to his characteristics or appearance.

Examples: Ayóó át'é.   - He is remarkable, great.
             Bizhé'égi át'é.   - He is like his father.

Nilį́, on the other hand, refers to the role a person plays.

Examples: Azee'iił'íní nilį́.   - He is a doctor.
             Bá'ólta'í nishłį́.   - I am a teacher.
             Áłchíní danohłį́.   - You (3+) are children.
             Ashkii yázhí nishłį́í ńt'ę́ę́'. - I was a little boy.
             Tábąąhá nilį́.   - She is of the Edge of the Water clan.

■ PRACTICE

A. Translate the following sentences into Navajo.

1. I am a doctor. _____

2. She is a teacher. _____

3. Who is a medicine man? _____

4. They are my grandmother and grandfather._____

5. He is my little brother. _____

6. She is my older sister. _____

7. They (3+) are her children. _____

8. I was a cowboy. _____

9. You (1) are the leader. _____

10. I am of the Bitter Water (Tódich'íí'nii) clan. _____

B. Answer the following questions.

1. Ha'át'íísh nílį? _____

2. Háíshą' bá ólta'í nilį? _____

3. Háísh nihinaat'áanii nilį? _____

4. Háísh azee'iił'íní nilį? _____

5. Siláo nílį́ísh? _____

6. Háísh ba'ałchíní danilį? _____

PATTERNS

One of the more common uses of the verb nilį is to tell what clan you are. When introducing one's self, there are four clans that should be identified. The clan system in matrilineal, or in other words, follows the lineage of mother. Notice how this is done.

Tábąąhá nishłį́.	- I am Edge of the Water clan (my mother's clan).
Bit'ahnii éí báshíshchíín.	- I am born for Under his Cover People clan (my father's clan which is my paternal grandmother's clan).
Nát'oh dine'é éí dashicheii	- My maternal grandfather is Tobacco People (which is his mother's -- my great grandmother's clan).
Kin yaa'áanii éí dashinálí	- My paternal grandfather is Towering House People (which is his mother's -- my great grandmother's clan).

The clan system is a very important part of Navajo society. There are many social expectations and taboos associated with other members of your clan. It is improper to date or marry someone from the same or related clan. When someone of the same clan is in need, it is expected that clan relatives should help out. For a more complete listing of relationships and clans, see Kinship Terms and Clans - Dóone'é on pages 143 through 146 in the Conversational Navajo Dictionary.

PRACTICE

Here are some questions that are in the form of a dialogue. They can help you practice concepts you've learned over the past several lessons.

1. Nicheii hólǫ́ǫ́sh?_____. Nimásáníshą'? _____. Haash wolyé? ____
_____. Dikwíísh binááhai? _____

Háádę́ę́' naa'aash? _____

Ninálísh hólǫ́? _____. Haash wolyé? _____

Éí háadi baghan? _____.

88

Nimá dóó nizhé'é haash wolyé? _____ Háadi baghan? _____ .

Éí dikwíí binááhai? _____ .

Na'áłchínísh hóló? _____ . At'ééké éí dikwíí? _____ .

Ashiikéshą' _____ . Haash daolyé? _____ .

Dikwíísh beedááhai? (plural form of binááhai) _____ .

2.   Now that you have answered too many questions, organize some of your responses into a paragraph telling about your family. You might also want to include informations about the number of sons or daughters, what they like or don't like, what they have, what their favorite food is, and some of their personality traits using state-of-being verbs. You'll be surprised at how much you can say!

_____
_____
_____
_____
_____
_____
_____
_____
_____
_____
_____
_____
_____
_____
_____
_____
_____
_____
_____
_____
_____
_____
_____
_____
_____

■ VOCABULARY BUILDER - EXPRESSIONS WITH NILÍ

Here are a few more expressions that can easily be learned using the verb nilį́.

dichin nishłį́	- I am hungry
dibáá' nishłį́	- I am thirsty
tsxį́įł nishłį́	- I am in a hurry
*bídin nishłį́	- I need it

*At this point we have not yet learned how to say this in the third person. It would be yídin nilį́. It will be explained later in discussing situations with a third person subject and a third person object.

■ PRACTICE

Using the verb nilį́ in conjunction with the above expressions, answer the following questions. Use a negative answer in some of your responses.

1. K'adísh dichin nílį? _____

2. Háísh dibáá' nilį? _____

3. Doósh tsxį́įł nílį́į da? _____

4. Béesoósh bídin nílį́į ńt'ę́ę́'? _____

5. Áłchínísh dichin danilį? _____

6. Nitsilísh tsxį́įł nilį? _____

7. Dibáá'ísh nílį? _____

8. Chidísh bídin nohłį́? _____

9. Doósh dichin nílį́į da? _____

10. Siláo tsxį́įł nilį́įsh? _____

LESSON 14 MORPHEMES - STEM AND SUBJECT MARKER

GRAMMAR

■   SOUND CHANGES

Say the following pairs of words and listen for the sound changes in the underlined letters.

permi<u>t</u>	- permi<u>ss</u>ion	ten<u>s</u>e	- ten<u>s</u>ion
conver<u>t</u>	- conver<u>s</u>ion	deci<u>d</u>e	- deci<u>s</u>ion
objec<u>t</u>	- objec<u>t</u>ion	conclu<u>d</u>e	- conclu<u>s</u>ion

Notice that when the suffix "-ion" is added to a verb (to change it to a noun), the sound of the final consonant changes. In English, sounds in different positions are modified, dropped, or replaced by other sounds. Changes like these also occur in Navajo. The sound changes that happen to morphemes in Navajo are very regular, which helps to simplify learning verbs.

> SOUND CHANGE: a sound is modified, dropped,
> or replaced by another sound.

■   PRACTICE

Identify which of the following words have undergone a sound change by writing "yes" or "no."

1.   shi + áchį́įh -----------> shíchį́įh   _____

2.   bi + łééchąą'í -----------> biłééchąą'í   _____

3.   ni + dziil -----------> nidziil   _____

4.   háá + di -----------> háadi   _____

5.   bi + aa -----------> baa   _____

■   VERB MORPHEME - STEM (POSITION 10)

Each Navajo verb, as you remember, is composed of morphemes which occur in particular morpheme positions. When morphemes are combined together, sound changes often occur.

Let's break down the verb *nilį́* into morphemes. First, the <u>stem</u>:

					STEM
nishłį́	=	nish	+		lį́
nílį́	=	ní	+		lį́
nilį́	=	ni	+		lį́
niidlį́	=	niid	+		lį́
nohłį́	=	noh	+		lį́

As you can see, the stem of "to be" is *lį́*. The stem contains the verb's basic meaning. Think of the stem as similar to Latin roots in English. It is the final syllable of the verb (without other suffixes) and occurs in position 10.

```
STEM:  morpheme in verb position 10 containing
       the basic meaning of the verb.
```

◼ PRACTICE

Write the stem of each verb in the blanks provided.

1. yíníshta' _____

2. naniné _____

3. wohcha _____

4. neiikai _____

5. hanishtá _____

◼ VERB MORPHEME - SUBJECT MARKER (POSITION 8)

Now let's break the verb down a bit more to find another verb morpheme. Remember that certain morphemes indicate what or who the subject of the verb is. These morphemes are called subject markers. Look at the following sentences.

I teach.   She is.
You eat.   We try.

In the above sentences, "I," "you," "she," and "we" are all subject markers. Following are some verb forms arranged according to the person and number of the subject. Try to discover what the subject markers are. (Hint: What morpheme is common to each verb in the group?)

FIRST PERSON SINGULAR	nish - łį	ash - hosh
	naash - né	iish - yeed
	yínísh - ta'	hash - ne'
SECOND PERSON SINGULAR	ní - łį	sodíl - zin
	hó - taał	kééhó - t'į
	íł - hosh	í - yą́
THIRD PERSON SINGULAR	ni - łį	yi- cha
	yoo - dlą́	a - yą́
	naa - né	hal - ne'

The first person singular marker is *sh* (notice the similarity to shí). The second person singular marker is a high tone. There is no marker for the third person -- it is absent or soundless. Now try to discover what the dual subject markers are in the examples below.

FIRST PERSON DUAL	niid - łį	yii - dlóóh
	kééhwii - t'į	ánii - t'é
	na'nii - tin	yii - dą́
SECOND PERSON DUAL	noh - łį	na'noh - tin
	woh - cha	doh - ní
	oh - dlą́	hoh - taał

The first person dual marker is *iid*. Often the d drops out due to a sound change. Finally, the second person dual marker is *oh*. These subject markers apply to many, but not all, Navajo verbs.

Now we can identify two morphemes in the verb *nilį́*.

nishłį́	=	ni	+	sh	+	łį́
nílį́	=	ni	+	í	+	łį́
nilį́	=	ni	+		+	łį́
niidlį́	=	ni	+	iid	+	łį́
nohłį́	=	ni	+	oh	+	łį́

SUBJECT MARKERS: (Position 8)		
	Singular	Dual
First Person	sh	iid
Second Person		oh
Third Person	none	

Write the subject marker of each verb in the first blank. Then write the English pronoun corresponding to the subject of the verb in the second blank.

1. na'nítkaad   _____   _____

2. dohní   _____   _____

3. hwiilne'   _____   _____

4. ashdlá   _____   _____

5. díínááł   _____   _____

6. niit'áázh   _____   _____

7. hohtaał   _____   _____

8. íyá   _____   _____

9. wolyé   _____   _____

10. ádeeshłííł   _____   _____

A final note about morphemes. Learning a few of the basic morphemes, specifically the stem and subject markers, can really help you in quickly learning other new verbs. You might have wondered why the plural forms of the subject markers were not discussed. Here's the reason. The subject markers for the plural forms are the same as the dual forms. The plural form of the verbs are indicated in Position 3 with the "da" plural marker. We will not spend much more time in learning the other morphemes. Now, let's get back to learning more conversational Navajo.

LESSON 15   AROUND THE SCHOOL

VOCABULARY

jooł	- ball
jooł iih nálniihí	- basketball
jooł yikalí	- baseball
jooł yitalí	- football
késhjéé'	- shoe game
tsidił	- stick dice
yéigo	- diligently
tł'óó'di	- outside
hoot'é	- an area is
ńchííl	- it is snowing
níyol	- it is windy
nizhónígo oo'ááł	- it is a nice day
yiizįįh	- stand up (singular)
daohsįįh	- stand up (plural)
dah ńdaah	- sit down (singular)
dah dinoohbįįh	- sit down (plural)
hágo	- come here
woshdéé'	- come this way
t'áadoo ánít'íní	- don't do that (knock it off)
naanish	- work
naalnish	- she is working
naané	- he is playing

PRACTICE

Practice the above vocabulary words until you can recite them from memory.

PATTERNS

The following phrases will help you talk about the student's favorite subject - recess. Since recess is usually outside, here are some simple weather phrases.

Question:	Tł'óó'di haash hoot'é?	How is it outside?
Answers:	Nizhónígo oo'ááł.	It is a nice day.
	Tł'óó'di deesdoi.	It is hot outside.
	Tł'óó'di deesk'aaz.	It is cold outside.
	Nahałtin.	It is raining.
	Ńchííl.	It is snowing.
	Níyol.	It is windy.

95

PRACTICE

Respond the the following questions. On yes-no questions, vary your answers by responding in both the positive and negative.

1. K'adshą' tłóó'di haa hoot'é? _____ _____

2. Tłóó'diish níyol? _____

3. Doósh ńchííl da? _____

4. Háadishą' nahałtin? _____

5. Tłóó'di deesk'aazísh? _____

6. Phoenixdiísh deesdoi? _____

7. Nizhónígo oo'ááł, ya'? _____

GRAMMAR

School seems to be all work or play, depending on whether you're the teacher or the student. Accordingly, here are two very useful verbs -- WORKING, TO BE and PLAYING, TO BE. They are very similar; the only exception is the classifier (position 9) and the stem (position 10 that defines the meaning).

WORKING, TO BE	SINGULAR	DUAL	PLURAL
FIRST PERSON	naashnish	neiilnish	ndeiilnish
SECOND PERSON	nanilnish	naałnish	ndaałnish
THIRD PERSON	naalnish		ndaalnish

Note: The WORK, TO BE verb has a "L" classifier, which means it has a "L" in position 9. It becomes silent after the "sh" subject marker, and a ł after the "oh" subject marker.

PLAYING, TO BE	SINGULAR	DUAL	PLURAL
FIRST PERSON	naashné	neii'né	ndeii'né
SECOND PERSON	naniné	naahné	ndaahné
THIRD PERSON	naané		ndaané

Note: The PLAY, TO BE verb has a 0 classifier. The glottal stop in 1st person dual and plural is a sound change where "iid" + né ----> ii'né. Try and say it; you'll see why it happens.

■ *Naalnish* (he is working)

Here are a number of ways in which the verb WORKING, TO BE can be used. It is found on page 129 in the Conversational Navajo Dictionary. First we'll use *naanish* (work) the nominalized (noun form) of the verb.

Question:	Naanish nił nantł'ahísh?	- Is work difficult for you?
Answer:	Aoo' naanish shił nantł'ah.	- Yes, work is difficult for me.
Answer:	Ndaga', naanish doo shił nantł'ah da.	- No, work is not hard for me.
Question:	Háísh naanish bił yá'át'ééh?	- Who likes work?
Answer:	Mary naanish bił yá'át'ééh.	- Mary likes work.
Question:	Naanishdi háísh bił hóyéé'?	- At work who is lazy?
Answer:	Naanishdi naat'áanii bił hóyéé'.	- At work the boss is lazy.
Question:	Naanishdi háísh bich'į' nahwii'ná?	- Who is having problems at work?
Answer:	Naanishdi shich'į' nahwii'ná.	- I am having problems at work.

Next, look at how the verb may be used in its conjugated form.

Question:	Háadishą' nanilnish?	- Where do you work?
Answer:	Ólta'di naashnish.	- I work at the school.
Question:	Háísh bił nanilnish?	- Who do you work with?
Answer:	Áłchíní bił naashnish.	- I work with children.
Question:	Ha'át'íísh binanilnish?	- What are you working on?
Answer:	Shaghan binaashnish.	- I'm working on my house.
Question:	Nichidísh naalnish.	- Does your car work?
Answer:	Ndaga', shichidí doo naalnish da.	- No, my car doesn't work.
Question:	Nimáásh doo naalnish da?	- Doesn't your mother work?
Answer:	Ndaga', shimá béeso bá hooghandi naalnish.	- No, my mother works at the bank.
Question:	Ha'át'íísh bee nanilnish?	- By means of what are you working? (as a tool)
Answer:	Bee atsidí bee naashnish.	- I am working by means of a hammer.

As you can see, there are a lot of situations in which this verb can be used. It can refer to a person working, working with them (in combination with *bił*), work on it (in combination with *bi-*), an object working (like a car), and working with it (as in working with a tool).

Answer the following questions.

1. Háadishą' nanilnish? _____

2. Háísh béeso bá hooghandi naalnish? _____

3. Ninaanishísh nił yá'át'ééh? _____

4. Áłchínísh bił nanilnish? _____

5. Doósh nichidí naalnish da? _____

6. Háísh ólta'di ndaalnish? _____

7. Háísh naanish bił yá'át'ééh? _____

8. Ha'át'íísh binanilnish? _____

9. Háísh naanish bił nantł'ah? _____

10. Naanishdi háísh doo yéigo naalnish da? _____

■ *Naané* (he is playing)

The following examples show how the verb PLAYING, TO BE can be used. It is found on page 97 in the Conversational Navajo Dictionary.

Question: Ha'át'íísh bee naniné?	- What are you playing?
Answer: Jooł bee naashné.	- I am playing ball.
Question: Fred háadi naané?	- Where is Fred playing?
Answer: Fred tł'óó'di naané.	- Fred is playing outside.
Question: Jooł yitalí bee ndaahnéésh?	- Are you (3+) playing football?
Answer: Ndaga', jooł yikalí bee ndeii'né.	- No, we're playing baseball.
Question: Tsidiłísh bee nihił naashné?	- Can I play stick dice with you?
Answer: Aoo', tsidił bee nihił naniné.	- Yes, play stick dice with us.

(Note: In this example two postpositions are used: the *bee* referring to its object "tsidił", and *nihił* referring to "with you".)

The verb PLAYING, TO BE can be used in a variety of ways. It can refer to playing, playing by means of it using the postposition *bee* (as a game, toy, or instrument), or with someone using the postposition *bił*.

PRACTICE

Answer the following questions.

1.   Háadi naniné? _____

2.   Ha'át'íísh bee ndaahné? _____

3.   Jooł yikalísh bee naniné? _____

4.   Háadishą' Karen naané? _____

5.   Háísh tł'óó'di naané? _____

6.   Yéigoósh naahné? _____

7.   Doósh tsidił bee naninée da? _____

8.   Háadi jooł yitalí bee ndeii'née dooleeł? _____

9.   Késhjéé'ísh bee naniné? _____

10. Háísh doo naanée da? _____

COMMON PHRASES

Below are some common phrases that are useful in the classroom.

yiiziih	- stand up (singular)
daohsiih	- stand up (plural)
dah ńdaah	- sit down (singular)
dah dinoohbiih	- sit down (plural)
hágo	- come here
woshdę́ę́'	- come this way (come in, as in a room)
t'áadoo ánít'íní	- don't do that (knock it off)

PRACTICE

Without looking at the above definitions, match the following phrases.

1. dah ńdaah	____ stand up (singular)
2. hágo	____ stand up (plural)
3. t'áadoo ánít'íní	____ sit down (plural)
4. yiiziih	____ come this way (come in, as in a room)
5. woshdę́ę́'	____ don't do that (knock it off)
6. dah dinoohbiih	____ sit down (singular)
7. daohsiih	____ come here

LESSON 16 AROUND THE SCHOOL PART 2

VOCABULARY

doo ajiníi da	- one doesn't say that	łeh	- ususally
doo ajít'įį da	- one doesn't do that	łahda	- sometimes
Diné bizaad	- Navajo language	t'áásáhígo	- individually
Nakaii bizaad	- Spanish language	ahił	- together
Bilagáanaa bizaad	- English language		
aseezį binaaltsoos	- newspaper		
ółta'	- he is reading		
yółta'	- she is reading it		
na'nitin	- he is teaching		
neinitin	- she is teaching them		

GRAMMAR

In this lesson we will learn the following two new verbs: HE IS READING/ HE IS READING IT andHE IS TEACHING/ HE IS TEACHING THEM. Observe the difference between the verbs listed below.

READING, TO BE	SINGULAR	DUAL	PLURAL
FIRST PERSON	íínishta'	ííníilta'	da'ííníilta'
SECOND PERSON	ííníłta'	íínółta'	da'íínółta'
THIRD PERSON	ółta'		da'ółta'

READING IT, TO BE	SINGULAR	DUAL	PLURAL
FIRST PERSON	yínishta'	yíníilta'	deíníilta'
SECOND PERSON	yíníłta'	yínółta'	deínółta'
THIRD PERSON	yółta'		dayółta'

Notice that the difference between the two verbs is that the second one has a direct object stated in the verb. This direct object "it" is in morpheme position 4. When using the verb, READING IT, TO BE, you must state what is being read, or in other words, you must state the direct object. This verb is called a Transitive verb, or one with a direct object. The verb READING, TO BE, however, does not have a direct object. It is an Intransitive verb.

Note: The "da" plural marker combines with the yí to form deí in a sound change.

100

■ Ólta' (he is reading)

Here are a number of ways that the verb READING, TO BE can be used. It is found on page 115 in the Conversational Navajo Dictionary under the listing of STUDY, TO.

Question:	Yéigoósh íínílta'?	- Are you diligently studying?
Answer:	Aoo', yéigo ííníshta'.	- Yes, I'm studying diligently.
Question:	Mary háadi ólta'?	- Where is Mary going to school?
Answer:	Mary Kinłánídi ólta'.	- Mary going to school at Flagstaff.
Question:	Háísh bił íínílta' łeh?	- Who do you studying with usually?
Answer:	Susan bił ííníshta' łeh.	- I study with Susan usually.
Question:	Dikwíidi íínílta'?	- What grade are you in?
Answer:	Ashdla'di ííníshta'.	- I am in the fifth grade.
Question:	Doósh íínólta' da?	- Aren't you(2) studying?
Answer:	Ndaga' , ííníilta'.	- No, we are studying.
Question:	Diné baa da'íínólta'ísh?	- Are you (3+) studying about the Navajos?
Answer:	Aoo' Diné baa da'ííníilta'.	- Yes, we are studying about the Navajos.

Notice that this verb can also be used to express going to school, to be studying, and to be in a grade level. The meaning may very depending on the context. Hence, the fifth example could mean, "Can you (2) read? " or "Are you (2) going to school?" A useful application of this verb is found in the fourth example. It can be used in combination with *dikwíidi?* - how many times, to refer to being in a certain grade level. In the last example, the postposition *baa* - about it, is used in combination with the verb to mean study about it.

■ Yólta' (he is reading it)

Next, let's look at the verb in its <u>transitive</u> form. Remember the transitive form indicates that a <u>direct object</u> is stated. This verb is found on page 101 of the Conversational Navajo Dictionary under the listing READ IT, TO. In the following examples, the <u>direct object</u> is underlined.

Question:	Abínígo <u>ha'át'iísh</u> yínílta' łeh?	- In the morning, <u>what</u> do you read usually?
Answer:	Abínígo, <u>aseezí binaaltsoos</u> yíníshta' łeh.	- In the morning, I read the <u>newspaper</u> usually.
Question:	Háísh <u>shinaaltsoos</u> yólta'?	- Who is reading my <u>book</u>?
Answer:	Joe <u>ninaaltsoos</u> yólta'.	- Joe is reading your <u>book</u>.
Question:	<u>Diné bizaad</u> yínílta'ísh?	- Do you read the <u>Navajo language</u>?
Answer:	Aoo', <u>Diné bizaad</u> yíníshta'.	- Yes, I read the <u>Navajo language</u>.

Question:	Háíshą' Bilagáanaa bizaad doo yółta' da?	- Who doesn't read English?
Answer:	Shicheii Bilagáanaa bizaad doo yółta' da.	- My grandfather doesn't read English.
Question:	Łahdaásh Nakaii bizaad yínította'?	- Sometimes do you read Spanish?
Answer:	Ndaga', Nakaii bizaad doo yíníshta' da.	- No, I don't read Spanish.
Question:	Áłchíní ha'át'íísh bich'į' yínította' łeh?	- What do you usually read to the children?
Answer:	Áłchíní binaaltsoos bich'į' yíníshta' łeh.	- I usually read children's books to them.

Notice that in each of the previous examples, the direct object is stated.

■ PRACTICE

Answer the following questions using positive and negative responses where appropriate.

1. Yéigoósh da'íínółta' łeh? _____

2. Łahdaásh Diné bizaad baa íínította'? _____

3. Háadishą íínółta' k'ad? _____

4. Dikwíidi íínította'? _____

5. Háísh doo ółta' da? _____

6. Háidí naaltsoos yínította'? _____

7. Ábínígoósh aseezį binaaltsoos yínította' łeh? _____

8. Háísh Naakaii bizaad dayółta'? _____

9. Łahdaásh Diné bizaad deínółta'? _____

10. Naaltsoosísh nihich'į' yínította'? _____

■ COMMON PHRASES

The following phrases are helpful in the classroom.

doo ájiníi da	- one doesn't say that
doo ájít'įį da	- one doesn't do that
t'áásáhígo da'íínółta'	- study individually
ahił da'íínółta'	- study together

Next we will learn the verbs TEACHING, TO BE and TEACHING HIM, TO BE which are found on page 117 of the Conversational Navajo Dictionary.

TEACHING, TO BE	SINGULAR	DUAL	PLURAL
FIRST PERSON	na'nishtin	na'niitin	nda'niitin
SECOND PERSON	na'nítin	na'nohtin	nda'nohtin
THIRD PERSON	na'nitin		nda'nitin

TEACHING HIM, TO BE	SINGULAR	DUAL	PLURAL
FIRST PERSON	nanishtin	naniitin	ndaniitin
SECOND PERSON	nanítin	nanohtin	ndanohtin
THIRD PERSON	neinitin		ndeinitin

These verbs are actually the same verb in the transitive and intransitive forms, similar to the pattern we used in the ółta' and yółta' verbs. The verbs na'nitin and neinitin, however, have one additional way of being used that is not usually found in other two. See if you can discover it in the next grammar concept.

◼ DELETION OF THE OBJECT PRONOUN *bi*

Remember that the third person object pronoun (him, her, or it) is *bi*. When the verb is transitive and uses an object pronoun as the direct object it is in morpheme position 4 in the verb. If the subject of the verb is in the first or second person, *bi* usually drops out of the verb.

Examples:

na	+	b̶i̶	+	nish	+	tin --------->	nanishtin
na	+	b̶i̶	+	ní	+	tin --------->	nanítin
na	+	*yi	+	ni	+	tin --------->	neinitin (na + yi ---> nei)
na	+	b̶i̶	+	nii	+	tin --------->	naniitin
na	+	b̶i̶	+	noh	+	tin --------->	nanohtin

This change only occurs with bi, not with the other object pronouns (shi, ni, nihi). Furthermore, it only occurs when the subject of the verb in in the first or second person, not when the subject is in the third person. When both the subject and the object are in the third person, a third-on-third situation exists, and the *bi* object pronoun changes to *yi*.

* This is a situation of a 3rd person subject acting on a 3rd person object, so the object pronoun *bi* changes to *yi*.

Unlike the verb TO READ IT, which only really uses the third person object *bi* (who needs to say "I am reading you?"), the object of the verb TO TEACH HIM may be changed to "me," or "you," or "us". Thus, you could say "I am teaching you," or "You are teaching us," or "He is teaching us," etc. Again, these pronouns are placed in object pronoun morpheme position 4.

> The object pronoun bi usually drops out of the verb when
> the subject of the verb is in the first or second person.
> The other object pronouns may be substituted to indicate
> a different direct object.

■ PRACTICE

Translate each of the following sentences to reflect a change in the object pronoun.

1. nanishtin - I am teaching him.
    I am teaching you (1). _____
    I am teaching you (3+). _____

2. nanítin - You (1) are teaching him.
    You are teaching me. _____
    You are teaching us. _____

3. nanohtin - You (2) are teaching him.
    You (2) are teaching me. _____
    You (2) are teaching us. _____

4. naniitin - We (2) are teaching him.
    We (2) are teaching you(1). _____
    We (2) are teaching you(3+). _____

5. neinitin - He is teaching him.
    He is teaching us. _____
    He is teaching you (3+). _____

6. ndeinitin - They (3+) are teaching him.
    They (3+) are teaching us. _____
    They (3+) are teaching me. _____

■ THE INDEFINITE OBJECT PRONOUN 'a

As you remember, the object pronoun in an action verb indicates the object ot the verb (the person or thing that is acted upon). Sometimes this object is definitely known, so a definite object pronoun (*shi, ni, nihi, bi, or yi*) is used. Sometimes, however, the object of the verb in not known. In these cases, the indefinite object pronoun 'a (someone, something) is used.

Compare the sentences below:

| nanihinishtin | = | na | + | nihi | + | nish | + | tin |
| na'nishtin | = | na | + | 'a | + | nish | + | tin |

Notice that while the literal meaning of na'nishtin is "I am teaching someone," it is usually translated into English as "I am teaching." As you can see, a sound change occurred when 'a was inserted in the verb above; the 'a dropped out and left only the glottal stop. This is what happened in the yółta'/ółta' verb we learned earlier.

> When the object of the verb is "someone" or "something,"
> insert the indefinite object pronoun 'a in the object pronoun
> position.

■ TO TEACH ABOUT IT

When the postposition *bee* (concerning it) is placed before the verb"to teach," or "to teach him," the meaning of the combination becomes "to teach [him] about it." *Bee* changes to *yee* in third-on-third situations. Often in English we leave out the word "about" and instead we say "to teach it." For example, we might say, "I teach math," or "I teach Navajo." Whether you are saying "I teach about it," or "I teach it, "you must include the postposition *bee* in Navajo.

Examples:

Diné bizaad bee na'nishtin.	- I teach (about) Navajo.
Mary Diné bizaad yee na'nitin.	- Mary is teaching (about) Navajo.
Diné bizaad bee nanihinishtin.	- I am teaching you (3+) about Navajo.

> To say "to teach about it" or "to teach him about it,"
> place *bee* (*yee* in third-on-third situations) before the verb.

A. Identify which of the following sentences require *bee (yee* in third-on-third) before the verb by writing Aoo' or Ndaga' in the blanks provided.

_____ 1. I am teaching children.

_____ 2. I am teaching the Navajo language.

_____ 3. You are teaching me.

_____ 4. They are teaching math.

_____ 5. We are teaching on the reservation.

_____ 6. What do you teach?

_____ 7. She teaches weaving.

_____ 8. He is teaching us Spanish.

B. Answer the following questions.

1.   Ha'át'íísh bee na'nítin? _____

2.   Háísh nanítin? _____

3.   Háísh Diné bizaad yee naninitin? _ _____

4.   Háadi na'nítin? _____

5.   Bilagáanaa bizaadísh bee na'nítin? _____

6.   Háísh Diné bizaad bee ndanohtin? _____

7.   Tł'éé'goósh na'nítin? _____

8.   Ha'át'íísh áłchíní bee nanítin? _____

9.   Łahdaásh ólta'di na'nítin? _____

10.   Háadishą' nda'nohtin łeh? _____

LESSON 17 GO VERBS - GOING, WENT, AND ARRIVED

VOCABULARY

Ch'ínílį	- Chinle, AZ
Na'nízhoozhí	- Gallup, NM
T'iisyaakin	- Holbrook, AZ
Tóta'	- Farmington, NM
Naat'áaniinééz	- Shiprock, NM
Tódinéeshzhee'	- Kayenta, AZ
Tónaneesdizí	- Tuba City, AZ
Tségháhoodzání	- Window Rock, AZ
kintah	- town
doogááł	- he will go
naayá	- he went and returned
níyá	- he arrived
dííshjį	- today
jį́įdą́ą́'	- earlier today
adą́ą́dą́ą́'	- yesterday
yiską́ągo	- tomorrow
hahosh (shą')	- when in the future
haadą́ą́' (shą')	- when in the past

   PRACTICE

Review the above vocabulary until you can recite them from memory.

GRAMMAR

   ADVERBS OF TIME

Adverbs of time are words like "yesterday," "tomorrow," and "in the morning." In addition to the adverbs of time listed in Lesson 9, here are a few more that you will find useful. Notice where they are used in the sentences below.

<u>Dííshjį</u> yéigo da'ííníilta'.	- Today we are studying diligently.
Béeso shee hólǫ́ǫ́ ńt'ę́ę́', <u>adą́ą́dą́ą́'</u>.	- I had money, yesterday.
<u>Yiską́ągo</u> Tóta'di naashnish dooleeł.	- Tomorrow I will be working at Farmington.
<u>Jį́įdą́ą́'</u> dichin nishłį́į́ ńt'ę́ę́'.	- Earlier this morning I was hungry.

Notice that the adverbs of time occur in the same positions that they do in English, either at the first or last of a sentence or phrase.

> Adverbs of time usually occur at the first or last of a sentence or phrase.

■ Doogááł (He will go, arrive)

The next "go verb" we will learn is doogááł (he will go, arrive). Doogááł is a future verb form. The singular stem of this verb is *gááł*; the dual stem is *'ash*; the plural stem is *kah*.

GO/ARRIVE, HE WILL	SINGULAR	DUAL	PLURAL
FIRST PERSON	deesháał	diit'ash*	diikah
SECOND PERSON	díínáał	dooh'ash	doohkah
THIRD PERSON	doogááł	doo'ash	dookah

The forms of doogááł have different meanings, depending on the directional suffixes that come before the verb. Look at the pair of sentences below.

T'iisyaakingóó diikah.   - We (3+) will go to Holbrook.
T'iisyaakindi diikah.   - We (3+) will arrive at Holbrook.

Notice that this verb can express two different ideas -- "to go" and "to arrive." One generally goes *to* a place using the suffix *-góó* (to). One arrives *at* a place using the suffix *-di*. Here are some examples of how this verb may be used in conversation.

Question: Yiskąągo háágóósh díínáał?
 - Tomorrow, where will you go?
Answer: Yiskąągo Naat'áaniinéézgóó deesháał.
 - Tomorrow I will go to Shiprock.

Question: Hahoshą' Sam Tódinéeshzhee'di doogááł?
 - When will Sam arrive at Kayenta?
Answer: Naaki yiskąągo Sam Tódinéeshzhee'di doogááł
 - In two days Sam will arrive at Kayenta.

Question: Na'nízhoozhígóósh doohkah?
 - Will you (3+) go to Gallup?
Answer: Aoo', Na'nízhoozhígóó diikah.
 - Yes, we will go to Gallup.

Question: Hahosh Tséghághoodzánídi doohkah?
 - When will you(3+) arrive at Window Rock?
Answer: Yiskąągo abíní, Tséghághoodzánídi diikah.
 - We (3+) will arrive at Window Rock tomorrow morning.

Question: Dííjįįgoósh béeso bá hooghangóósh dooh'ash?
 - Will you (2) go to the bank today?
Answer: Ndaga', yiskąągo béeso bá hooghangóó diit'ash.
 - No, tomorrow we (2) will go to the bank.

Note: An interesting sound change occurs here on the stem. The *iid* subject marker combines with the *'ash* stem to form *iit'ash*. Try it; you'll find the *iid'ash* is pronounced *iit'ash*!

108

Answer the following questions.

1.   Yiską́ą́go háágóósh díínáał? _____

2.   Hahosh Lucy Ch'íníłį́góó doogą́ą́ł? _____

3.   Hahoshą' Tónaneesdizídi doohkah? _ _____

4.   Háísh Tóta'góó doogą́ą́ł? _____

5.   Díí tł'éé'goósh hooghangóósh dooh'ash? _____

■   Naayá (he went and returned)

Another "go verb" is naayá (he went and returned). Notice that it has the same three stems as the verb deeyá.   It is the perfective form of the verb naaghá.

HE WENT AND RETURNED	SINGULAR	DUAL	PLURAL
FIRST PERSON	nséyá	nshiit'áázh	nsiikai
SECOND PERSON	nsíníyá	nshoo'áázh	nsoohkai
THIRD PERSON	naayá	naazh'áázh	naaskai

Naayá is used to express making a round trip (going and returning). It implies that you have already returned. In contrast, the verb níyá (which we will learn next) is used to express a one-way trip. Try to discover which directional suffix is used with the verb naayá.

Háágóósh nsíníyá?	- Where did you go <u>to</u> (and have now returned)?
Naalyéhé bá hooghangóó nséyá.	- I went <u>to</u> the trading post.
Háádą́ą́' Tóta'góó nsoohkai?	- When did you go <u>to</u> (and have now returned) Farmington?
Adą́ą́dą́ą́' Tota'góó nsiikai.	- We went <u>to</u> (and have now returned) Farmington yesterday.
Háísh kintahgóó naayá?	- Who went <u>to</u> (and has now returned) town?
Joe kintahgóó naayá.	- Joe went <u>to</u> town.

Notice that the -góó (to, towards) is used with naayá, just as "to" is used in the corresponding English sentences.

Translate the following sentences.

1.   I went to the school. _____

2.   We (3+) went to Holbrook. _____

3.   They (3+) went to town. _____

4.   You (2) went to the bank. _____

5.   Where did you (1) go? _____

Answer the following questions.

1.   Ni dóó nimá háágóósh nshoo'áázh? _____

2.   Adą́ą́dą́ą́' kintahgóósh nsíníyá? _____

3.   Jį́į́dą́ą́' háísh da'iigis bá hooghangóó naayá? _____

4.   Háádą́ą́' Tóta'góó nsoohkai? _____

5.   Nimá dóó nizhé'é ch'iyáán bá hooghangóósh naazh'áázh? _____

    _____

■   Níyá (he came, arrived)

The verb *níyá* (he came, arrived) has the same three stems as the verb *deeyá* and *naayá*. This verb is the perfective form of the future verb *doogááł*.

HE CAME, ARRIVED	SINGULAR	DUAL	PLURAL
FIRST PERSON	níyá	niit'áázh	niikai
SECOND PERSON	yíníyá	noo'áázh	noohkai
THIRD PERSON	níyá	ní'áázh	yíkai

Compare the following sentences in each group below to see how the verb *níyá* is used.
    1. Ólta'déé' níyá   - I came <u>from</u> the school.
    2. Ólta'di níyá.   - I arrived <u>at</u> the school.

1. Tóta' déé' noohkai.   - You (3+) arrived <u>from</u> Farmington.
2. Tóta'<u>di</u> noohkai.   - You (3+) arrived <u>at</u> Farmington.

Notice that the forms of *níyá* can express either the idea of "to come" or "to arrive," depending on which directional suffix precedes the verb. One comes from and arrives at a place. The suffix *-déé'* (from) precedes this verb to express the idea of "to come from" while the *-di* (at) precedes it to give the meaning of "to arrive at."

■ PRACTICE

A. Translate the following sentences.

1.   I arrived at the school. _____

2.   We (2) came from Gallup. _____

3.   They (3+) arrived at home. _____

4.   Who (1) arrived at the bank? _____

5.   When (in the past) did you (3+) arrived from Kayenta? _____

B. Answer the following questions.

1.   Háádą́ą́' Na'nízhoozhídę́ę́' noo'áázh? _____

2.   Abínídą́ą́' háísh ólta'di níyá? _____

3.   Adą́ą́dą́ą́' Ch'ínílį́dę́ę́' noohkaiísh? _____

4.   Háádę́ę́' yíníyá? _____

5.   Jį́į́dą́ą́' háísh kintahdi ní'áázh? _____

■ COMING TO PEOPLE

As we just learned, the verb níyá can mean "to come." Together with the postposition "-aa" (to), they can express the idea of coming to people. Look at the following examples, especially noting the postpositional phrases underlined.

John <u>shaa</u> níyá.   - John came <u>to me</u>.
John <u>naa</u> níyá.   - John came <u>to you</u>.
John <u>nihaa</u> níyá.   - John came <u>to us</u>.

<u>Shaa</u> noo'áázh.	- You (2) came <u>to me</u>.
<u>Nihaa</u> noo'áázh.	- You (2) came <u>to us</u>.
<u>George baa</u> noo'áázh.	- You (2) came <u>to George</u>.
<u>Naa</u> niit'áázh.	- We (2) came <u>to you (1)</u>.
<u>Nihaa</u> niit'áázh.	- We (2) came <u>to you (2+)</u>.
<u>Henry baa</u> niit'áázh.	- We (2) came <u>to Henry</u>.
Joe <u>shaa</u> doogááł.	- Joe will come <u>to me</u>.
Joe <u>naa</u> doogááł,	- Joe will come <u>to you (1)</u>.
Joe <u>nihaa</u> doogááł.	- Joe will come <u>to us</u>.
<u>Naa</u> deesháál.	- I will come <u>to you (1)</u>.
<u>Nihaa</u> deesháál.	- I will come <u>to you (2+)</u>.
<u>Sam baa</u> deesháál.	- I will come <u>to Sam</u>.

Notice that the verb tells who came, while the postposition tells who was visited. Do <u>not</u> overgeneralize using this combination. It can only be used with these two verbs - *níyá* and *doogááł*. It <u>doesn't</u> mean the same when used with the verb *naayá*, *naaghá*, or *deeyá*. Rather than meaning to come to someone or visiting someone, it may mean to molest them. The *-aa* postposition in combination with *naayá* or *naaghá* refers to "be doing."

> To express the idea of coming to someone, place a postpositional phrase with the postposition *-aa* before the verb *níyá* or *doogááł*.

■ PRACTICE

Translate the following sentences.

1. Yesterday he came to me. _____

2. We (3+) came to Jim. _____

3. My mother came to us. _____

4. You (3+) came to me. _____

5. They (3+) came to us. _____

6. I will visit my mother. _____

7. My father and mother will visit us. _____

8. We (3+) will visit you (3+). _____

9. You (2) will visit me. _____

10. They (3+)will visit us tomorrow. _____

LESSON 18 FORMING NOUNS

VOCABULARY

hataałii	- medicine man (singer)
bá ólta'í	- teacher
na'niłkaadii	- herder
azee' iił'íní	- doctor
bee ak'e elchíhí	- pencil
bik'i dah asdahí	- chair
bikáá' adání	- table
da'adání	- cafeteria
-í	- the one that
-ii	- the particular one that
-ígíí	- the one that; the particular one; the fact that; that which

■   PRACTICE

Practice the above vocabulary words until you can recite them from memory.

GRAMMAR

■   *-í* and *-ii* FORMING NOUNS

In English, many nouns are formed by adding a suffix to a verb (e.g. teach + er = teacher, play + er = player). Many nouns in Navajo are formed in this way. Try to discover the pattern by looking at the examples below.

bá ólta' + í	bá ólta'í
for him studying is done	teacher
da'adą́ + í	da'adání
eating is being done	cafeteria
bee ak'e elchí + í	bee ak'e elchíhí
by it writing is done	pencil, pen
bik'i dah asdá + í	bik'i dah asdáhí
on it sitting is done	chair
hataał + ii	hataałii
he sings	medicine man, singer

113

Notice that the suffixes -í and -ii change verbs (usually third person verb forms) into nouns in much the same way "-er" changes verbs into nouns in English. Now look at the previous verbs which end in a nasalized or high toned vowel. Notice that when they are combined with these suffixes, a sound change occurs; either n or h is inserted between the vowel and the suffix. If the final vowel is nasalized, n is inserted before the í or ii (as in *da'adání*). If the final vowel is high toned, then an h is inserted before the í or ii (as in *bee ak'e alchíhí*). If the word ends in a consonant or a low toned vowel, the í or ii is simply added to the word (as is hataałii).

> To form a noun, add the suffix -í or the suffix -ii to a verb.
> If the verb ends in a nasal vowel, insert n before the suffix.
> If the verb ends in a high toned vowel, insert an h before the suffix.

■ PRACTICE

Change each of the following verbs into a noun, then write the new definition.

	VERB	NOUN	NEW DEFINITION
1.	yá'át'ééh		
2.	łikan		
3.	hataał		
4.	na'nitin		
5.	naané		
6.	hólǫ́		
7.	hózhǫ́		
8.	bééhózin		
9.	nizhóní		
10.	nahalin		
11.	át'é		
12.	ílį́		
13.	nishłį́		
14.	diniih		
15.	neezgai		

114

-ígíí FORMING NOUN PHRASES

The suffix -ígíí is similar to the suffixes -í and -ii that we just learned. The suffix -ígíí is attached to verbs or sentences to form noun phrases. Look at the examples below and try to discover the meaning of -ígíí.

Angie Wilson wolyéhígíí	- the one that is called Angie Wilson
bił hózhónígíí	- the one that is happy
bitah hodiniihígíí	- the one that is aching all over
shaa ní'áázhígíí	- the fact that they two came to me.
shił bééhózinígíí	- that which I know
bił nantł'ahígíí	- that which is difficult for him

Notice that -ígíí can be attached either to a verb or a whole sentence to form a noun phrase. Depending on the context in which it is used, ígíí can mean "the one that...," "the particular one," "the fact that," "or "that which." When adding the -ígíí to the end of a word, use the same rules as when addind -í or -ii.

> To form a noun phrase, attach the suffix -ígíí (the one that, the particular one, the fact that, or that which) to the end of a verb or sentence.

PRACTICE

Change each of the verbs or sentences into a noun phrase and write it in the blank provided. Then write the translation of the new noun phrase.

NOUN PHRASE

1. ch'iyáán łikan _____

Translation: _____

2. nihaa níyá _____

Translation: _____

3. dichin nilį _____

Translation: _____

4. shichidí át'é _____

Translation: _____

5. hastiin dikos bidoolna' _____

Translation: _____

6. Áłchíní nanishtin _____

Translation: _____

7. Jooł bee naashné _____

Translation: _____

115

FORMING NEGATIVE NOUN PHRASES

Look at the examples below and try to discover what happens when the negator doo ... of doo...da is placed before the verb of a noun phrase or a noun formed with -ígíí, -í, or -ii.

Examples: doo nantł'ahígíí   - the one that is not difficult
ch'iyáán doo łikanígíí   - the food that does not taste good
doo shił bééhózinígíí   - that which I do not know
doo yá'át'ééhii   - not good ones

Non-examples: ~~doo yá'át'ééh daígíí~~
                 ~~doo łikan daígíí~~

As you can see, putting doo before the verb in a noun phrase formed with -ígíí or a noun formed with either -í or -ii converts it into a negative noun phrase. Notice from the non-examples that when forming negative noun phrases, the da of the combination doo...da is not used.

> To form a negative noun phrase, place the negator doo
> before the verb in a phrase that ends with -ígíí, -í, or -ii.

PRACTICE

Change each of the nouns or noun phrases below into a negative noun phrase and write it in the blank provided. Then below it write the new meaning.

NEGATIVE NOUN PHRASE

1. shił bééhózinígíí _____

Translation: _____

2. dichin nishłínígíí _____

Translation: _____

3. Diné bizaad bił nantł'ahígíí _____

Translation: _____

4. Ashkii bidziilígíí _____

Translation: _____

5. Mary nihaa níyáhígíí _____

Translation: _____

6. Béeso shee hólónígíí _____

Translation: _____

7. Ólta'di naashnishígíí _____

Translation: _____

8. Fred baa hoolzhiizhígíí _____

Translation: _____

LESSON 19 ADVERBS AND ADVERBIAL CLAUSES

VOCABULARY

damóo (go)	- (on) Sunday; week
damóo biiskání (go)	- (on) Monday
naaki jį́ nda'anish (go)	- (on) Tuesday
tágí jį́ nda'anish (go)	- (on) Wednesday
dį́į' jį́ nda'anish (go)	- (on) Thursday
nda'iiníísh (go)	- (on) Friday
damóo yázhí (go)	- (on) Saturday
náádamóogo	- next week
ńdeezid	- month
nááhai	- year
-yę́ędą́ą́'	- at that time in the past; last...
yiskánídą́ą́'	- days ago
azlį́į'go	- it has occurred

■ PRACTICE

Practice the above vocabulary words until you can recite them from memory.

■ PATTERNS - EXPRESSIONS OF TIME

The following phrases can help you talk about time.

1. number yiską́ągo   1. in number days
    naaki   two
    táá'   three

2. number yiskánídą́ą́'   2. number days ago
    dį́į'   four
    naaki   two

3. number damóo azlį́į'go   3. in number weeks
    táá'   three
    ashdla'   five

4. number _____-yę́ędą́ą́'   4. number _____ ago
              damóo   weeks
              ńdeezid   months (past)
              nááhai   years (past)

117

Translate the following phrases.

1.   in four days   _____

2.   five years ago   _____

3.   in two weeks   _____

4.   ten days ago   _____

5.   two months ago   _____

6.   in three days   _____

7.   four days ago   _____

8.   three months ago _____

9.   in four weeks   _____

10. six days ago   _____

GRAMMAR

■   -go   FORMING ADVERBS

We have used the suffix *-go* in several different situations previously. Let's take a look at how we can use to form adverbs. Try to discover its use in the examples below.

Yá'át'ééhgo na'nítin.	You (1) teach well.
Nizhónígo hataał.	He sings nicely.
Bił hózhǫ́ǫgo naané.	She is happily playing.
Díí naaltsoos shił nantł'ahgo yíníshta'.	I am reading this book with difficulty.

As you can see, *-go* can change a state-of-being verb such a *yá'át'ééh* and *nizhóní* into adverbs. One of its functions is like "-ly" in English.

> To form an adverb, add *-go* to a state-of-being verb.

PRACTICE

Change each of the following state-of-being verbs into adverb by adding the *-go*.

1. yá'át'ééh _____

2. nizhóní _____

3. hólǫ́ _____

4. łikan _____

5. nahalin _____

6. át'é _____

7. ádin _____

8. hodiniih _____

9. nantł'ah _____

10. neezgai _____

-go FORMING ADVERBIAL CLAUSES

We will now learn how tho use the suffix -go in making complex sentences (sentences with more than one verb). Try to discover how this is used by examining the sentences below.

Nahałtingo shił yá'át'ééh.	- <u>When</u> it is raining, I like it.
Shitah honeezgaigo doo shił hózhǫ́ǫ da.	- <u>While</u> I am sick, I am not happy.
Níyolgo doo tł'óó'di neiit'aash da.	- <u>When</u> it is windy, we don't go outside.
Ch'iyáán ádingo, dichin niidlį́.	- The food <u>being</u> gone , we are hungry.

Notice that -go is used to form groups of words such as *nahałtingo* (when it is raining) or *shitah honeezgaigo* (while I am sick). These word groups are called adverbial clauses. Adverbial clauses are useful in making complex sentences. Look below at some adverbial clauses with -go and the complex sentences in which they are used.

Adverbial Clause	Complex Sentence
Ólta'di neiikaigo When we're at school	Ólta'di neiikaigo, Diné bizaad deíníilta'. When we're at school, we study Navajo.
Tł'óó'di nahałtingo When it is raining	Tł'óó'di nahałtingo doo neii'née da. When it is raining, we don't play.

119

Shich'į' nahwii'náago   Shich'į' nahwii'náago ííníshta' łeh.
When I'm having problems   When I'm having problems, I usually study.

Béeso shee hólǫ́ǫgo   Béeso shee hólǫ́ǫgo, Tóta'góó deesháał.
When I have money   When I have money, I will go to Farmington.

> To form an adverbial clause, attach the suffix -go to a verb.

◼ PRACTICE

Translate the following. Then add a second clause to it to make a complex sentence.

1.   When it snows, _____
Complex sentence: _____

2.   When you study, _____
Complex sentence: _____

3.   While she is working, _____
Complex sentence: _____

4.   When he caught a cold, _____
Complex sentence: _____

5.   When he is being mischevious, _____
Complex sentence: _____

6.   When my grandmother is ill, _____
Complex sentence: _____

7.   When I have no money, _____
Complex sentence: _____

8.   When it rains and is windy, _____
Complex sentence: _____

9.   When I teach children, _____
Complex sentence: _____

10.   When I will go to Gallup, _____
Complex sentence: _____

■ -go FORMING "IF" CLAUSES

Try to determine another use of the suffix -go from the sentences below.

Diné bizaad yíníłta'go nił bééhózin dooleeł.
If you study Navajo, you will know it.

Dikos nidoolna'go nitah honeezgai łeh.
If you have a cold, you usually hurt all over.

Shimá shaa doogááłgo, Tségháhoodzánígóó diit'ash.
If my mother comes to see me, we will go to WindowRock.

Nizhónígo oo'ááłgo, tł'óó'di ndaahné.
If it's a nice day, play outside.

Notice that -go can also mean "if." With this meaning, it is used to form clauses, such as *Diné bizaad yíníłta'go* (if you study Navajo), that are conditional. We will call these dependent clauses "if clauses." When forming dependent "if clauses," attach -go to a verb and comes at the end to the clause.

> Dependent "if clauses" are formed by attaching -go to a verb.

■ PRACTICE

Translate the following. Then form a dependent "if clause" from each of the sentences below.

1. We (3+) are studying diligently. _____

2. Your grandmother will visit you. _____

3. You teach at night _____

4. You (3+) are playing baseball _____

5. Her name is Angie _____

6. You (1) work at the school _____

7. They (3+) like ice cream _____

8. Navajo is difficult for him _____

9. She is teaching them English _____

10. It is hot in Tuba City _____

■ doo ... góó FORMING NEGATIVE ADVERBIAL CLAUSES

So far we have learned how to form adverbial clauses and "if clauses" with the suffix -go.
Look at the examples below to discover how negative adverbial and "if clauses" are formed.

doo ńchíílgóó	- if it isn't snowing
doo dichin nílį́įgóó	- if you are not hungry
chidí doo nee hólǫ́ǫgóó	- if you don't have a car
díí doo shił łikangóó	- if this doesn't taste good to me

Non-examples:
   ~~doo ńchííl dago~~
   ~~doo dichin nílį́į dago~~

Notice that doo ... -góó is used to form negative adverbial clauses. Da of doo ... da is not
included in the negative clauses. This combination of the negator doo and the suffix góó
means "if not," "when not," "while not," or "as not." Look now at some complex sentences that
contain the above negative clause.

Doo ńchíílgóó shił hózhǫ́.
- I am happy when it is not snowing.

Doo dichin nílį́įgóó éí yá'át'ééh.
- When you are not hungry, it is good.

Chidí doo nee hólǫ́ǫgóó doo kintahgóó díínááł da.
- If you don't have a car, you will not go to town.

Díí doo shił łikangóó dichin nishłį́į dooleeł.
- If this doesn't taste good to me, I will be hungry.

As you can see, in forming negative clauses, doo precedes and -góó follows the verb or
postposition-verb combination.

> To form a negative adverbial or "if clauses," place doo before
> and -góó after a verb or postposition-verb combination.

■ PRACTICE

Form a negative adverbial clause from each of the sentences below; then complete the complex
sentence.

1.   Nił hózhǫ́. _____

2.   Béeso shee hólǫ́ _____

3.   Dikos nidoolna'. _____

4.   Áłchíní nanítin. _____

5.   Tł'óó'di niyol. _____

6.   Yéigo da'íínółta'. _____

7.   Jooł bee naniné. _____

8.   Bił hózhǫ́. _____

9.   Shitah hodiniih. _____

10. Tł'éé'go nanilnish. _____

◼ PATTERNS

Below is a listing of the days of the week. Notice that the -go suffix attached to the day refers to "on" or "being." Page 139 in the Conversational Navajo Dictionary gives alternate forms.

damóo (go)	- (on) Sunday; week
damóo biiskání (go)	- (on) Monday
naaki jí nda'anish (go)	- (on) Tuesday
tágí jí nda'anish (go)	- (on) Wednesday
dį́į' jí nda'anish (go)	- (on) Thursday
nda'iiníísh (go)	- (on) Friday
damóo yázhí (go)	- (on) Saturday

The word *damóo* (sometimes pronounced *damį́igo*) originated from the Spanish term for Sunday *domingo*. The word *biiskání* in Monday means "its tomorrow." The word *nda'anish* means work is done; hence, Tuesday is *naaki jí nda'anish* or the second day of work. Friday, being the last day of the work week is *nda'iiníísh*, or work is over. Saturday is the "little Sunday." Really, it makes more sense than the English (Greek) days of the week: Sunday, Moonday, Zeusday,* Mercuryday, Thorsday, *Venusday, Saturnday. *German translations of these give us Wednesday and Friday. Now, back to Navajo.

◼ PRACTICE

Translate the following sentences.

1.   On Friday, I will go to Holbrook. _____

2.   On Tuesday, what are we going to be doing? _____

3.   On Saturday, we are going to be playing baseball. _____

4.   On Sunday, we will go to church. _____

5.   On Wednesday, I don't work at the school. _____

123

LESSON 20 CONJUNCTIONS

VOCABULARY

dóó	- and	dootł'izh	- it is blue/green
áádóó	- and then	łichíí	- it is red
áko	- so	łitso	- it is yellow
ndi	- but	łibá	- it is gray
ákondi	- however	łizhin	- it is black
índa	- then	łigai	- it is white
háálá	- because	t'óóbaa'ih	- it is dirty
azhá...ndi	- even though	nineez	- it is long; tall
doodago	- or	ndaaz	- it is heavy
		sik'az	- it is cold
		sido	- it is hot

■ PRACTICE

Practice the above vocabulary words until you can recite them from memory.

GRAMMAR

■ PREDICATE NOMINATIVES (ENGLISH) VS. STATE OF BEING VERBS (NAVAJO)

When describing something or someone in English, we often use adjectives. Often in a sentence the adjective comes after the verb "to be" or another linking verb. At other times, the adjective comes before the noun.

> The car is <u>red</u>.
> The man is <u>heavy</u>.
> It is <u>hot</u>.
> The clothes are <u>dirty</u>.

In Navajo, there are very few adjectives. In their place, state-of-being verbs are used to describe objects or people. Look at examples of these verbs below.

> Chidí łichíí'.   - The car is <u>red</u>.
> Hastiin ndaaz.   - The man is <u>heavy</u>.
> Sido.   - It is <u>hot</u>.
> Éé' t'óóbaa'ih.   - The clothes are <u>dirty</u>.
> Non-examples:
>   Chidí łichíí' ~~át'é~~.
>   Hastiin ndaaz ~~át'é~~.
>   Éé' t'óóbaa'ih ~~át'é~~.

124

Many of the Navajo verbs that are used in place of adjectives are listed in the Conversational Navajo Dictionary. Here are the verbs that we will now learn.

t'óóbaa'ih	- it is dirty; filthy
ndaaz	- it is heavy
nineez	- it is long; tall
sik'az	- it is cold
sido	- it is hot

Examples:

Shikee' t'óóbaa'ih	- My shoes are dirty.
Chidí ndaaz.	- The car is heavy.
Díí bee ak'e alchíhí nineez.	- This pencil is long.
Abe' yistiní sik'az.	- The ice cream is cold.
Atoo' ayóó sido.	- The stew is very hot.

> In Navajo, state-of-being verbs take the place of predicate adjectives. There is no form of the verb "to be" included with the verb.

■ PRACTICE

Translate the following sentences.

1. This book is heavy. _____

2. My chair is cold. _____

3. The sheep is very heavy. _____

4. Your coat is filthy. _____

5. The water is hot. _____

6. The pencil is long. _____

7. My feet are cold. _____

8. His forehead is hot. _____

9. His pants are dirty. _____

10. My father is tall. _____

125

VOCABULARY BUILDER - COLORS

The verbs used to describe colors in Navajo function exactly like the state-of-being verbs we just learned. Remember that *át'é* does not follow these verbs.

dootł'izh	- it is blue/green
łichíí'	- it is red
łitso	- it is yellow
łibá	- it is gray
łizhin	- it is black
łigai	- it is white

Examples:

Shinaaltsoos dootł'izh.	- My book is blue.
Ńléí chidí łichíí'	- That car over there is red.
Díí ké łitso.	- These shoes are yellow.
Shi'éé'tsoh łibá.	- My coat is gray.
Nilééchąą'í łizhin.	- Your dog is black.
Shidéíji'éé' łigai.	- My shirt is white.

PRACTICE

Answer the following questions.

1. Háísh bichidí łitso? _____

2. Ni'éé'tsoh łizhinísh? _____

3. Naghan łibáásh? _____

4. Háísh bitł'ízí łigai? _____

5. Nináá' dootł'izhísh? _____

6. Háísh bi'éé' łichíí'? _____

LINKING WORDS - CONJUNCTIONS

Look at the following sentences.

Shimásání dibé bił yá'át'ééh <u>ndi</u> tł'ízí doo bił yá'át'ééh da.
My grandmother likes sheep <u>but</u> she doesn't like goats.

<u>Azhą́</u> shich'į' nahwii'náa <u>ndi</u>, shił hózhǫ́.
<u>Even though</u> I have problems, I am happy.

Tł'óó'di ńchííl; <u>ákondi</u> kóne'é deesdoi.
Outside it is snowing; <u>however</u>, in here it is hot.

126

Nihich'iyáán ádin, <u>áko</u> nihimá dóó nihizhé'é kintahgóó deezh'áázh.
We have no food, <u>so</u> our mother and father are going to town.

Shi'niidlí <u>háálá</u> shikee' ádin.
I'm cold <u>because</u> I have no shoes.

The underlined words in the sentences above link two sentences of phrases together. Except for *azhą́ ... ndi* (even though), they are used the same as their English counterparts. *Azhą́ ... ndi* is split up just like *doo ... da*, with the *azhą́* preceding the phrase and *ndi* following the phrase. Below are some common linking words.

dóó	- and
áko	- so
ndi	- but
ákondi	- however (possibly áko-so/ndi-but, similar to how/ever)
doodago	- or (literally "if not")
háálá	- because
azhá ... ndi	- even though

■ PRACTICE

Combine the following sentences using linking words. Use a variety of conjunctions.

1. Diné bizaad shił nantł'ah. Yéigo yíníshta'.

_____

2. Nihideiji'éé' ádin. Doo nihi'niidlíi da.

_____

3. Shich'į' nahwii'ná. Shił hózhǫ́.

_____

4. Ch'ééh déyá. Kintahgóó ńséyá.

_____

5. Tseebíidi oolkił. Dichin nishłį́.

_____

6. Abe' yistiní shił łikan. Nímasii doo shił łikan da.

_____

7. Béeso shee hólǫ́. Éé' ałdó' shee hólǫ́.

_____

Translate the following sentences using conjunctions.

1. I like cake but I don't like ice cream.

_____

2. My mother feels ill; however, my father is healthy.

_____

3. Even though he has money, he is not happy.

_____

4. Spanish is difficult for me so I am learning Navajo.

_____

5. It's cold outside; however it is hot in here.

_____

6. I am going to Gallup because my brother is there.

_____

7. Even though I am hungry, I am diligenty studying Navajo.

_____

8. It is now noon so I am hungry.

_____

9. I am going to Gallup or I am going to Farmington.

_____

10. Are you studying English or Navajo?

_____

ANSWER KEY TO PRACTICE QUESTIONS

The following answers are examples of how the questions in the practice execises may be answered. Recognize that there are countless other possible answers; these examples demonstrate possible answer patterns. Use your imagination.

LESSON 1

Page 27
1. Garth Wilson yinishyé.
2. Harrison wolyé.

Page 30
1. car under it
2. story about it
3. me toward
4. teacher with
5. her concerning

LESSON 2

Page 39
1. shi'niidlí.
2. nihiyooch'ííd.
3. bidziil.
4. Henry bóhólnííh.
5. ni'ádílááh (ne'ádílááh).
6. naat'áanii bóhólnííh.
7. nihijéékał.
8. Mary bits'iiní.
9. shijéékał.
10. dabidziil.
11. nihi'niidlí.
12. niyooch'ííd.
13. Mike bi'ádílááh (be'ádílááh).
14. **Shits'iiní.**

Page 40
1. Tanya ayóó bi'niidlí.
2. John íiyisíí bi**jéékał.**
3. Naat'áanii ayóó biyooch'ííd.
4. Bá'ólta'í ayóó bits'iiní.
5. T'áá íiyisíí shijéékał.
6. James ayóó bidziil.
7. Naat'áanii íiyisíí bóhólnííh.
8. Mark ayóó bi'ádílááh.

Page 41
1. John bidziil.
2. Bá'ólta'í bits'iiní.
3. Shí, shidziil.
4. Mary biyooch'ííd.
5. Naat'áanii bóhólnííh.
6. Mary bi'niidlí.
7. Ni, nijéékał.
8. Fred bi'ádílááh.
9. Arnold ayóó bidziil.

10. Louise íiyisíí bits'iiní.
11. Mark t'áá íiyiíí biyooch'ííd.
12. Larry ayóó bijéékał.
13. Martha íiyisíí bóhólnííh.
14. Shí, t'áá íiyisííshi'niidlí.
15. Ni, ayóó nijéékał.
16. Alvin íiyisíí bi'ádílááh.

LESSON 3

Page 43
1. bi'niidlíísh
2. bi'ádílááhísh
3. biyooch'íídísh
4. bijéékałísh
5. bits'iiníísh
6. bóhólnííhísh
7. dikos bidoolna'ísh (sometimes pronounced *ásh* because of the final *a* sound)
8. dichinísh bi'niiłhí
9. dichinísh bi'niigháá'
10. dibáá'ásh bi'niiłhí
11. dibáá'ásh bi'niigháá'

Page 44
1. doo bi'niidlíi da.
2. doo bidziil da.
3. doo ayóó bi'ádílááh da.
4. doo íiyisíí biyooch'ííd da.
5. doo ayóó bijéékał da.
6. doo t'áá íiyisíí bits'iiní da.
7. doo bóhólnííh da.
8. doo dikos bidoolna' da.
9. doo dichin bi'niiłhíi da.
10. doo dichin bi'niigháá' da.

Page 45
1. Ashkii ayóó bi'ádílááhísh?
+ Aoo', ashkii ayóó bi'ádílááh.
- Ndaga', ashkii doo ayóó bi'ádílááh da.

2. Asdzáán íiyisíí bijéékałísh?
+ Aoo', asdzáán íiyisíí bijéékał.
- Ndaga', asdzáán doo íiyisíí bijéékał da.

3. At'éédísh dikos bidoolna'?
+ Aoo', at'ééd dikos bidoolna'.
- Ndaga' at'ééddoo dikos bidoolna' da.

4. Hastiinísh dibáá' bi'niiłhí?
+ Aoo', hastiin dibáá' bi'niiłhí.
- Ndaga', hastiin doo dibáá' bi'niiłhíi da.

5. Ashkii dóó at'ééd dichinísh bi'niighą́ą́'?
+ Aoo', ashkii dóó at'ééd dichin bi'niighą́ą́'.
- Ndaga', ashkii dóó at'ééd doo dichin bi'niighą́ą́' da.

6. Asdzą́ą́nísh dikos bidoolna'?
+ Aoo', asdzą́ą́n dikos bidoolna'.
- Ndaga', asdzą́ą́n doo dikos bidoolna' da.

7. Hastiin dóó asdzą́ą́n dibáá'ásh bi'niighą́ą́'?
+ Aoo', hastiin dóó asdzą́ą́n dibáá' bi'niighą́ą́'.
- Ndaga', hastiin dóó asdzą́ą́n doo dibáá' bi'niighą́ą́' da.

8. Háísh doo dikos bidoolna' da? Ashkii doo dikos bidoolna' da.
9. Háíshą' doo íiyisíí bijéékał da? Mary doo íiyisíí bijéékał da.
10. Háí doo biyooch'įįd da? Shí, doo shiyooch'įįd da.
11. Háíshą' doo ayóó bidziil da? Asdzą́ą́n doo ayóó bidziil da.
12. Íiyisíí dichin ni'niiłhį́įsh? Aoo', íiyisíí dichin shi'niiłhį́.
13. Naat'áaniiísh íiyisíí bóhólnííh? Ndaga', naat'áanii doo íiyisíí bóhólnííh da.

LESSON 4
page 48
1. Háágóósh dishoo'áázh? Hooghangóó deet'áázh.
2. Henry háágóó deeyá? Henry ólta'góó deeyá.
3. Háísh naalyéhé bá hooghangóó deeyá? Mary naalyéhé bá hooghangóó deeyá.
4. Háágóóshą' deeskai? Béeso bá hooghangóó deeskai.
5. Háísh doo da'iigis bá hooghangóó deeyáa da? Lisa doo da'iigis bá hooghangóó deeyáa da.

page 49
1. Ch'ééh déyá.
2. Doo ch'ééh deeyáa da
3. Ch'ééh díníyáásh?
4. Ch'ééh deeskai ndahalin.

page 50
1. Háádę́ę́' naniná? Blandingdę́ę́' naashá.
2. Naat'áanii háádę́ę́' naaghá? Naat'áanii Shiprockdę́ę́' naaghá.
3. Háádę́ę́' naah'aash? Farmingtondę́ę́' neiit'aash.
4. Háísh Phoenixdę́ę́' naaghá? Lucy Phoenixdę́ę́' naaghá.
5. Flagstaffdę́ę́' nanináásh? Aoo', Flagstaffdę́ę́' naashá. Ndaga', doo Flagstaffdę́ę́' naasháa da.
6. Háádę́ę́' naakai? Tuba Citydę́ę́' naakai.

LESSON 5
page 52
1. Mary dóó Helen ńléidi naa'aash.
2. Lee ńléidi naaghá.
3. Kodi neiit'aash.
4. Aoo' Mark áadi naaghá.
5. Ashiiké aadi naakai.

page 53
1. shinaat'áanii
2. ninaaltsoos
3. nihi'éé'

131

page 53
4. bibéeso
5. bikee'
6. bich'iyáán
7. nihighan
8. shinaaltsoos
9. nihibéeso
10. nihikee'

LESSON 6

page 56
1. Naaltsoos yá'ádaat'ééh. Past: Naaltsoos yá'ádaat'ééh ńt'éé'.
   Future: Naaltsoos yá'ádaat'ééh dooleeł.
2. Shibéeso hóló̧. Past: Shibéeso hóló̧o̧ ńt'éé'. Future: Shibéeso hóló̧o̧ dooleeł.
3. Nihich'iyáán ádin. Past: Nihich'iyáán ádin ńt'éé'.
   Future: Nihich'iyáán ádin dooleeł.
4. Bi'éé' át'é. Past: Bi'éé' át'éé ńt'éé'. Future: Bi'éé' át'ee dooleeł.
5. Nichidí shichidí nahalin. Past: Nichidí shichidí nahalin ńt'éé'.
   Future: Nichidí shichidí nahalin dooleeł.
6. Shina'ídíkid hóló̧. Past: Shina'ídíkid hóló̧o̧ ńt'éé'.
   Future: Shina'ídíkid hóló̧o̧ dooleeł.
7. Nichidí yá'át'ééh. Past: Nichidí yá'át'ééh ńt'éé'.
   Future: Nichidí yá'át'ééh dooleeł.
8. Binaaltsoos ádin. Past: Binaaltsoos ádin ńt'éé'.
   Future: Binaaltsoos ádin dooleeł.
9. Háísh bikee' át'é? Past: Háísh bikee' át'éé ńt'éé'.
   Future: Háísh bikee' át'ee dooleeł.
10. Ni'éé' bi'éé' nahalin. Past: Ni'éé' bi'éé' nahalin ńt'éé'.
    Future: Ni'éé' bi'éé' nahalin dooleeł.
11. Ha'át'íísh át'é? Past: Ha'át'íísh át'éé ńt'éé'? Future: Ha'át'íísh át'ee dooleeł.

LESSON 7

page 59
1. shich'į'   nihich'į'
   nich'į'   nihich'į'
2. shaa   nihaa
   naa   nihaa
3. shee   nihee
   nee   nihee

page 60
1. shaa
2. nich'į'
3. nihił
4. nihaa
5. bee
6. shee
7. nił
8. shich'į'
9. baa
10. naa

132

page 60
1. Mary bił
2. Henry baa
3. hastiin bee
4. asdzáán bich'į'

page 62
1. Aoo', chidí shee hóló.
2. Ndaga', naaltsoos doo shił yá'át'ééh da.
3. Aoo', diné bizaad shił nantł'ah.
4. Larry déíji'éé' bee ádin.
5. Bilagáanaa bizaad shił bééhózin.
6. Ashkii tł'aaji'éé' bee hóló.
7. Béeso doo shił yá'át'ééh da.
8. Hastiin doo bił hózhǫǫ da.
9. Aoo', éé'tsoh shee hóló.
10. Physics shił nantł'ah.
11. Shimá dibé bee hóló.
12. Diné bizaad doo shił bééhózin da.
13. Ndaga', k'ad doo shił hózhǫǫ da.

page 64
1. nihee dahóló
2. bee ádaadin
3. nihił yá'ádaat'ééh
4. bił dahózhǫ
5. nihił ndantł'ah
6. nihił béédahózin

page 64
1. Béeso nihee dahóló.
2. Aoo', chidí nihee **dahóló.**
3. Ndaga', diné bizaad doo nihił ndantł'ah da.
4. Aoo', ólta' nihił yá'ádaat'ééh.
5. Bilagáanaa doo bił dahózhǫǫ da.
6. Quantum physics nihił béédahózin.

LESSON 8
Page 67
1. Eii tsésǫ' át'é.
2. Eii shibéeso át'ée dooleeł.
3. Ndaga' ńléí at'ééd doo nizhóní da.
4. Aoo', éí dibé tł'ízí nahalin.
5. Díidí chidí ayóó shił yá'át'ééh.
6. Díí John bilééchąą'í át'é.
7. Ndaga', łééchąą'í doo shee hólǫǫ da.
8. Shidó', diné bizaad shił nantł'ah.
9. Eiidí tł'aaji'éé' doo shił nizhóní da.
10. Aoo', eii shidéíji'éé' át'é.

page 77

1. Naalyéhé bá hooghandi ké nahaniih.
2. Naadiin béeso bą́ą́h ílį́.
3. Farmingtondi éé' nahaniih.
4. Éé' ashdla'áadah béeso bą́ą́h ílį́.
5. Ch'iyáán bá hooghandi nahaniih.
6. Chidí bitoo' t'ááłá'í béeso bą́ą́h ílį́.
7. Dibé hastą́diin béeso bą́ą́h ílį́.
8. Flagstaffdi chidí nahaniih.
9. Neeznáá béeso shee hólǫ́.
10. Shichidí naadiindi mííl bą́ą́h ílį́ ńt'ę́ę́'.

LESSON 11
page 79

1. + Aoo', bááh shił łikan. - Ndaga' bááh doo shił łikan da.
2. + Aoo', bilasáanaa shił łikan. - Ndaga' bilasáanaa doo shił łikan da.
3. + Hashk'aan shił łikan. - Atsį' doo shił łikan da.
4. + Aoo', atsį' dóó nímasii shił łikan.
   - Ndaga', atsį' dóó nímasii doo shił łikan da.
5. Shimá ch'ééh jiyáán doo bił łikan da.

page 79

1. Abe' shaa níkaah.
2. Nímasii shaa níkaah.
3. Bilasáanaa shaa ní'aah.
4. Dah diníilghaazh shaa níkaalı.
5. Ashįįh shaa ní'aah.

LESSON 12
page 83

1. Shibid neezgai.
2. John bikee' diniih.
3. Aoo', shiwoo' diniih.
4. Ndaga', shíla' doo neezgai da.
5. Aoo' shijaa' diniih.
6. Hastiin bił nahodééyá.
7. Aoo', ashkii chin bą́ą́h ádin.
8. Asdzáán doo bitah honeezgai da.
9. Aoo', hastiin biyi' hodilid.
10. Ndaga', asdzáán doo bą́ą́h dahaz'ą́ą da.

page 85

1. + Aoo', hashk'aan doo shił łikan da.
   - Ndaga', hashk'aan shił łikan.
2. + Aoo', doo ch'ééh déyáa da.
   - Ndaga', ch'ééh déyá.
3. + Aoo', díí chidí doo shił nizhóní da.
   - Ndaga', díí chidí shił nizhóní.
4. + Aoo', béeso doo shee hólǫ́ǫ da.
   - Ndaga', béeso shee hólǫ́.
5. + Aoo', naaltsoos doo shił yá'át'ééh da.
   - Ndaga', naaltsoos shił yá'át'ééh.
6. + Aoo', k'ad doo baa hoolzhiizh da.
   - Ndaga', k'ad baa hoolzhiizh.

7. + Aoo', shizhé'é doo nahalin da.
- Ndaga' shizhé'é nahalin.
8. + Aoo', diné bizaad doo shił bééhózin da.
- Ndaga', diné bizaad shił bééhózin.
9. + Aoo', doo shitah yá'áhoot'ééh da.
- Ndaga', shitah yá'áhoot'ééh.

LESSON 13

page 87

1. Azee' iił'íní nishłį́.
2. Bá'ólta'í nilį́.
3. Háísh hataałii nilį́.
4. Shicheii dóó shimásání nılį́.
5. Shitsilí nilį́.
6. Shádí nilį́.
7. Ba'áłchíní danilį́.
8. Akałii nishłį́į́ ńt'ę́ę́'.
9. Naat'áanii nílį́.
10. Tódich'íí'nii nishłį́.

page 88

1. Bá'ólta'í nishłį́.
2. Henry bá'ólta'í nilį́.
3. Bill nihinaat'áanii nilį́.
4. Kathy azee' iił'íní nilį́.
5. Ndaga', doo siláo nishłį́į da.
6. Lucille ba'áłchíní danilį́.

page 88

1. Aoo', shicheii hólǫ. Shimásánídó' hólǫ. Joseph dóó Louisa wolyé. Shicheii éí tseebíídiin binááhai dóó shimásání éí tsosts'idiin dóó ba'aan hastą́ą́ binááhai. Gallupdę́ę́' naa'aash. Shinálí ałdó' hólǫ. Fred dóó Mary wolyé. K'ad éí Flagstaffdi baghan. Shimá éí Martha wolyé dóó shizhé'é éí Harold wolyé. Farmingtondi baghan. Shimá éí ashdladiin dóó ba'aan ashdla' binááhai doo shizhé'é éí hastą́diin binááhai. Aoo', sha'áłchíní hólǫ. At'ééké éí naaki. Kim dóó Danielle wolyé. Ashiiké éí naaki ałdó'. Joe dóó Sam wolyé. Kim éí táá' binááhai doo Danielle éí ashdla' binááhai. Joe éí naakits'áadah binááhai dóó Sam éí tseebíí binááhai. Sha'áłchíní danizhóní.

page 90

1. Aoo', k'ad dichin nishłį́.
2. Larry dibáá' nilį́.
3. Aoo', doo tsxį́į́ł nishłį́į da.
4. Aoo' béeso bídin nilį́į ńt'ę́ę́'.
5. Ndaga', ałchíní doo dichin danilį́į da.
6. Aoo', shitsilí tsxį́į́ł nilį́.
7. Ndaga' doo dibáá' nishłį́į da.
8. Aoo', chidí bídin niidlį́.
9. Ndaga' dichin nishłį́.
10. Aoo', siláo tsxį́į́ł nilį́.

LESSON 14

page 91

1. yes
2. yes
3. no
4. yes
5. yes

page 92

1. ta'
2. né
3. cha
4. kai
5. tá

page 94

1. ´ you 1
2. oh you 2+
3. iid we 2+
4. sh I
5. ´ you 1
6. iid we 2+
7. oh you 2+
8. ´ you 1
9. none he/she/it
10. sh me

LESSON 15

page 96

1. K'ad tł'óó'di nizhónígo oo'ááł.
2. Ndaga', tł'óó'di nahałtin.
3. Aoo', doo ńchííl da.
4. Shiprockdi nahałtin.
5. Aoo', tł'óó'di deesk'aaz.
6. Ndaga' Phoenixdi deesk'aaz.
7. Aoo', nizhónígo oo'ááł.

page 98

1. Ólta'di naashnish.
2. Shimá béeso bá hooghandi naalnish.
3. Aoo', shinaanish ayóó shił yá'át'ééh.
4. Ndaga', doo ałchíní bił naashnish da.
5. Aoo', shichidí doo naalnish da.
6. Bá'ólta'í ólta'di ndaalnish.
7. Hataałii binaanish bił yá'át'ééh.
8. Shichidí binaashnish.
9. Shádí naanish bił nantł'ah.
10. Naanishdi naat'áanii doo yéigo naalnish da.

page 99

1. Tł'óó'di naashné.
2. Jooł bee ndeii'né.
3. Ndaga', jooł yikalí doo bee naashnée da.
4. Ólta'di Karen naané.
5. John tł'óó'di naané.

6. Aoo', yéigo neii'né.
7. Ndaga', tsidił bee naashné.
8. Ólta'di jooł yitalí bee ndeii'née doo.
9. Aoo', késhjéé' bee naashné.
10. Fred doo naanéé da.

1-7: 4,7,6,5,3,1,2

LESSON 16

1. Aoo', yéigo da'íníílta' łeh.
2. Aoo', diné bizaad baa íínίshta' łahda.
3. Hooghandi ííníilta' k'ad.
4. Ashdla'di íínίshta'.
5. Shimá doo ólta' da.
6. Díí naaltsoos yínίshta'.
7. Aoo', abínígo aseezį binaaltsoos yínίshta' łeh.
8. Shicheii Naakai bizaad yółta'.
9. Aoo', Diné bizaad deíníilta' łahda.
10. Ndaga', doo naaltsoos nihich'į' yínίshta' da.

1. naninishtin / nanihinishtin
2. nashinίtin / nanihinίtin
3. nashinohtin / nanihinohtin
4. naniniitin / nanihiniitiin
5. nanihinitin / nanihinitin
6. ndanihinitiin / ndashinitin

1. ndaga'
2. ndaga'
3. ndaga'
4. aoo'
5. ndaga'
6. ndaga'
7. aoo'
8. aoo'

1. Diné bizaad bee na'nishtin.
2. Áłchíní nanishtin.
3. Hastiin Benally Diné bizaad yee nashinitin.
4. Ólta'di na'nishtin.
5. Ndaga', Bilagáanaa bizaad doo bee na'nishtin da.
6. Áłchíní Diné bizaad bee ndaniitin.
7. Ndaga', abínígo na'nishtin.
8. Áłchíní Bilagáanaa bizaad bee nanishtin.
9. Aoo', łahda ólta'di na'nishtin.
10. Hooghandi nda'niitin łeh.

LESSON 17

page 109

1. Yiską́ągo Tóta' góó deesháá̱ł.
2. Naaki yiską́ągo Lucy Ch'ínílígoo doogááł.
3. Díí tł'éé'go Tónaneesdizídi diikah.
4. Shimá Tóta'góó doogááł.
5. Ndaga', yiską́ągo hooghangóó diit'ash.

page 110

1. Ólta'góó nséyá.
2. T'iisyaakingóó nsiikai.
3. Kintahgóó naaskai.
4. Béeso bá hooghangóó nshoo'áázh.
5. Háágóóshą' nsíníyá?

page 110

1. Shí dóó shimá ch'iyáán bá hooghangóó nshiit'áázh.
2. Ndaga', jį́į́dą́ą́' kintahgóó nséyá.
3. Jį́į́dą́ą́' shimá da'iigis bá hooghangóó naayá.
4. Adą́ą́dą́ą́' Tóta'góó nsiikai.
5. Aoo', shimá dóó shizhé'é ch'iyáán bá hooghangóó naazh'áázh.

page 111

1. Ólta'di níyá.
2. Na'nízhoozhídę́ę́' niit'áázh.
3. Hooghandi yíkai.
4. Háísh béeso bá hooghandi níyá.
5. Háádą́ą́' Tódinéeshzhee'dę́ę́' noohkai.

page 111

1. Jį́į́dą́ą́' Na'nízhoozhídę́ę́' niit'áázh.
2. Abínídą́ą́' ashkii ólta'di níyá.
3. Aoo', adą́ą́dą́ą́' Ch'ínílį́dę́ę́' niikai.
4. Da'iigis bá hooghandę́ę́' níyá.
5. Jį́į́dą́ą́' Mary dóó Jim kintahdi ní'áázh.

page 112

1. Adą́ą́dą́ą́' shaa níyá.
2. Jim baa niikai.
3. Shimá nihaa níyá.
4. Shaa noohkai.
5. Nihaa yíkai.
6. Shimá baa deesháá̱ł
7. Shimá dóó shizhé'é nihaa doo'ash.
8. Nihaa diikah.
9. Shaa dooh'ash.
10. Yiską́ągo nihaa dookah.

LESSON 18

page 114

1. yá'át'óóhii/ thc good one
2. łikaní/ the delicious one
3. hataałii/ the singer
4. na'nitiní/ the one who teaches
5. naanéhé/ the one who plays

140

1. Shí, shichidí łitso.
2. Ndaga', shi'éé'tsoh łibá.
3. Ndaga' shaghan łichíí'.
4. Shicheii bitł'ízí łigai.
5. Aoo', shináá' dootł'izh.
6. Shádí bi'éé' łichíí'.

1. Diné bizaad shił nantł'ah, áko yéigo yíníshta'.
2. Nihidéíji'éé' ádin ndi doo nihi'niidlíi da.
3. Azhą́ shich'į' nahwii'náa ndi shił hózhǫ́.
4. Ch'ééh déyá háálá kintahgóó ńséyá.
5. Tseebíidi oolkił áko dichin nishłį́.
6. Abe' yistiní shił łikan ákondi nímasii doo shił łikan da.
7. Béeso shee hólǫ́ dóó éé' ałdó' shee hólǫ́.

1. Bááh łikaní shił ndi abe' yistiní doo shił łikan da.
2. Shimá bitah honeezgai ákondi shizhé'é bitah yá'áhoot'ééh.
3. Azhą́ bibéeso hólǫ́ǫ ndi doo bił hózhǫ́ǫ da.
4. Naakai bizaad shił nantł'ah áko Diné bizaad yíníshta'.
5. Tł'óó'di deesk'aaz ákondi kone'é deesdoi.
6. Na'nízhoozhígóó deesháál háálá shitsilí áadi naaghá.
7. Azhą́ dichin nishłį́į ndi Diné bizaad yéigo yíníshta'.
8. K'ad ałní'ní'ą́ áko dichin nishłį́.
9. Na'nízhoozhígóó deesháál éí doodago Tóta'góó deesháál.
10. Bilagáanaa bizaadísh éí doodago Diné bizaadísh yíníłta'?